Teacher's Edition

Maps Globes Graphs

Level F

Contents

About the Program T2
Scope and Sequence T4
Introduction to the Five Themes of Geography T6
Teaching Strategies T7
Blackline Masters
   Letters to Families T24
   Map Attack! T26
   Map of the United States T27
   Map of North America T28
   Map of South America T29
   Map of Europe T30
   Map of Africa T31
   Map of Asia T32
   Map of Australia and the South Pacific T33
   Map of the Eastern and Western Hemispheres T34
   Robinson Projection Map of the World T35
   Standardized Midterm Test T36
   Standardized Final Test T38
Test Answer Key T40

Meet your state standards with free blackline masters and links to other materials at:
www.HarcourtAchieve.com/AchievementZone
Click Steck-Vaughn Standards

ISBN 0-7398-9112-X

© 2004 Harcourt Achieve Inc.

9 10 11 12 13 14 15   1678   17 16 15 14 13 12
4500351826

Rigby • Steck-Vaughn

www.HarcourtAchieve.com
1.800.531.5015

About the Program

Steck-Vaughn *Maps•Globes•Graphs* has been developed to teach important geography and social studies skills in a six-level program. Up-to-date, in-depth information in a self-contained format makes this series an ideal supplement to basal texts or an excellent independent social studies skills course. Clear, concise maps present new concepts in a straightforward manner without overwhelming students with too much information. As students develop practical skills, such as map interpretation, they also develop the confidence to use these skills. The features incorporated into the *Maps•Globes•Graphs* program were developed to achieve these goals.

Maps•Globes•Graphs consists of six student books with accompanying annotated Teacher's Editions. The series is organized as follows:

Book	Level
Level A	Grade 1
Level B	Grade 2
Level C	Grade 3
Level D	Grade 4
Level E	Grade 5
Level F	Grade 6

STUDENT EDITION FEATURES

◆ **Consistent formats** for each chapter include two teaching pages that introduce the skill, two practice pages, one mixed practice page, and *Skill Check*, a review page.

◆ **Geography Themes Up Close** introduces the five themes of geography—location, place, human/environment interaction, movement, and regions—in the beginning of the book. These themes are reinforced in five two-page special features that emphasize the concepts and relevance of the themes.

◆ *Map Attack!* and *Graph Attack!* features (in the three upper-grade books) build general understanding of interpreting map and graph information in a step-by-step format.

◆ **Vocabulary** words highlighted in bold type emphasize in-context definitions and increase understanding of the terms critical to studies in geography.

◆ **Glossaries** in each student book serve as both an index and a resource for definitions of key terms.

◆ **Atlas maps** in each book are a valuable reference tool for instruction and study.

TEACHER EDITION FEATURES

◆ **Annotated** Teacher's Editions facilitate effective instruction with minimal preparation.

◆ **Scope and Sequence** reflects key concepts of basal instruction for each grade level.

◆ **Teaching strategies** identify key objectives and vocabulary for each chapter and provide suggestions for introducing skills, teaching specific lesson pages and concepts, following up lessons with extension activities, and enhancing concept mastery with activities to complete at home.

◆ **Extension activities** involve both cooperative learning and critical thinking, and reinforce the concepts and skills taught in the program.

◆ **Geography themes teaching strategies** reinforce geography skills and vocabulary through lesson introductions, teaching notes, and extension activities.

◆ **Blackline masters** further supplement the activities available for use:

Map Attack! may be used with maps in a basal text or in reference materials.

Outline maps appropriate to each grade level may be used for skills practice in map labeling and place recognition.

Activities and *games* reinforce concepts.

Standardized tests in each level allow students to check their learning, as well as practice test-taking skills.

Steck-Vaughn Company grants you permission to duplicate enough copies of these blacklines to distribute to your students. You can also use these blacklines to make overhead transparencies.

◆ **Transparencies** provide full-color instructional aids. These transparencies may be used to introduce lessons, to reinforce key map and globe skills, or to review chapter concepts. These transparencies are perforated in the back of the teacher's editions for easy removal.

◆ **Letters to Families,** in English and in Spanish, are provided in each book. The letters invite families to participate in their child's study of the book and provide suggestions for some specific activities that can extend the concepts presented in the program.

SUGGESTIONS FOR PROGRAM USE

Maps•Globes•Graphs is easy to implement in any classroom. The following suggestions offer ways to adapt the program to particular classroom and student needs.

◆ Alternate the *Maps•Globes•Graphs* chapters with chapters in the social studies program. After presenting your first social studies chapter, present the first chapter of *Maps•Globes•Graphs*. When you return to the regular social studies program, apply any map skills learned to maps that appear in the curriculum. In this way, students reinforce their new skills in a variety of contexts.

◆ Set aside a specific time each week for map study. For example, spend half an hour every Friday on map study. Do as much in the *Maps•Globes•Graphs* Worktext® as time permits. Related activities, such as map show and tell, could be included in the map study time.

◆ Focus on a complete chapter of map study and cover the entire program at the beginning of the year, at the end of the year, or whenever best fits your class schedule.

The map and globe chapters in *Maps•Globes•Graphs* progress developmentally. For this reason they should be taught in the order they are presented in the Worktext®. However, the last chapter in each book presents several types of graphs, so this chapter could be interspersed with map chapters. In Levels D, E, and F, the graph topics reflect subjects covered by the maps and the basal programs. The graphs also can be used in conjunction with the graph presentation in mathematics studies.

Meet your state standards with free blackline masters and links to other materials at **www.HarcourtAchieve.com/AchievementZone**. Click **Steck-Vaughn Standards**.

Scope and Sequence

Numbers refer to the chapters where each skill is first taught. These skills are reviewed and reinforced throughout the book and the series, as well as in the "Geography Themes Up Close" special features.

		LEVEL A	LEVEL B	LEVEL C	LEVEL D	LEVEL E	LEVEL F
Map Recognition	Photo/Picture Distinction	1, 2					
	Photo/Map Distinction	3	2		1		
	Map defined	3	2	1	1		2
Map Key/Legend	Pictorial symbols/Symbol defined	6	2	1	1	2	
	Labels	7	7	1	1	2	2
	Legend defined and related to map	6	2	1	1	2	2
	Abstract symbols		2, 3, 6	1, 3	1	2	2
	Political boundaries		6	1	1	2	2
Direction	Top, Bottom, Left, Right	4					
	North, South, East, West	5	3	1	1	1	1
	Relative location	4–7	3–6	1–6	1–8	1–5, 7, 8, 11	2–5, 10
	Compass rose		3	1	1	1	2
	Cardinal directions (term)				1	1	2
	Intermediate directions			1	2	1	2
Scale and Distance	Miles/Kilometers/Map Scale/Distance			2	4	3	3
	Mileage markers				5	4	4
Latitude and Longitude	Equator		4	7	7	8	1, 6
	Latitude			7	7	8	6
	Degrees			7, 8	7	8	6
	Longitude/Prime Meridian			8	8	9	6
	Estimating Degrees				7	8, 9	6
	Parallel					8	6
	Meridian					9	6
	Latitude and Longitude					9	6
The Globe	Globe	7	4	7, 8	7, 8	1	1
	North Pole/South Pole		4	8	7, 8	1, 8–10	1
	Continents/Oceans		4, 5	7, 8	7, 8	8, 9	1
	Northern/Southern Hemispheres			7	7	8	1
	Eastern/Western Hemispheres			8	8	9	1
	Tropics of Capricorn/Cancer					8	7
	Arctic/Antarctic Circles					8	7

		LEVEL A	LEVEL B	LEVEL C	LEVEL D	LEVEL E	LEVEL F
Grids	Grid Coordinates/Map index			6	3	7	4
Graphs	Pictograph			9			
Graphs	Bar Graph			9	9	12	12
Graphs	Line Graph			9	9	12	12
Graphs	Circle Graph			9	9	12	12
Graphs	Time Line			9	9		
Graphs	Flow Chart			9	9		
Graphs	Tables					12	12
Landforms	Types of Landforms		1	4	6	5	5
Landforms	Landform Maps			4			
Landforms	Relief Maps				6	5	5
Landforms	Physical Maps/Elevation					5	5
Types of Maps	Route Maps			5	5	4	4
Types of Maps	Resource Maps			3	1		9
Types of Maps	Special Purpose Maps				1	6	8, 9
Types of Maps	Combining Maps/Comparing Maps						8, 9
Types of Maps	Historical Maps					6	
Types of Maps	Climate Maps						7, 8
Types of Maps	Land Use Maps						9
Types of Maps	Inset Maps		7			3	3
Time Zones	Time zones defined					11	10
Time Zones	International Date Line						10
Temperature Zones	Low latitudes					10	7
Temperature Zones	Middle latitudes					10	7
Temperature Zones	High latitudes					10	7
Temperature Zones	Sun/Earth relationship					10	7
Projections	Projections defined						11
Projections	Mercator						11
Projections	Robinson						11
Projections	Polar						1, 11

Geography Themes

OBJECTIVES

Students will
- identify the five geographic themes: location, place, human/environment interaction, movement, and regions
- describe the absolute and relative location of their school
- recognize the physical and human features of places
- give examples of how people interact with the environment
- identify movement of people, goods, information, and ideas
- recognize and give examples of regions and their features

VOCABULARY

geography	human/environment
location	interaction
place	movement
physical features	regions
human features	

INTRODUCING THE FIVE THEMES OF GEOGRAPHY

- In 1984 a joint committee of the National Council for Geographic Education and the Association of American Geographers published the *Guidelines for Geographic Education: Elementary and Secondary Schools*. This publication outlined the five fundamental themes in geography—location, place, human/environment interaction, movement, and regions. These themes help geographers and geography students organize the information they gather as they study Earth and its people.
- **Location** is the position of people and places on Earth. Location is described in two ways—absolute location and relative location. Absolute location is described using a specific address based on a grid system. Latitude and longitude is the absolute location of a place based on the intersection of lines of latitude and lines of longitude. Relative location describes a location in relation to what it is near or what is around it. One way of using relative location is by giving directions. How would you tell a friend to get to your house from the local library? The special feature about location is on pages 48 and 49.
- **Place** is described by two kinds of features—physical features and human features. Physical features include such natural features as landforms, altitude, climate, soil, and plant and animal life. Human features include population, housing, the economy, how people make a living, the language,

religious beliefs, customs, and ways of life. The special feature about place is on pages 34 and 35.
- **Human/Environment Interaction** describes the interaction of people and their environment—how people adapt to or change their environment. For example, people in areas with earthquakes adapt to the environment by using special building materials to help withstand the effects of earthquakes. Farmers change the environment by clearing the land of trees in order to grow crops. The special feature about human/environment interaction is on pages 62 and 63.
- **Movement** describes the ways that people, goods, information, and ideas move from one part of Earth to another by way of transportation and communication. This theme also includes the reasons for migration and the cause-and-effect relationships of movement. The study of movement helps geographers understand why people settled in places. The special feature about movement is on pages 20 and 21.
- **Regions** are the basic units of geographic study. Geographers use various features to classify a place as a region. Some physical features used include climate, landforms, natural resources, and vegetation. Some human features include cultural beliefs, language, government, and economics. A region has common characteristics. A region can be as small as a neighborhood or as large as a continent. A region can change as its features change. For example, changes in political status, population distribution, or standards of living can cause the region to change. The special feature about regions is on pages 76 and 77.

TEACHING NOTES

Pages 4–7 Read and discuss the activities with students. Point out that students will learn more about the five themes of geography in special features called "Geography Themes Up Close."

EXTENSION ACTIVITIES

- As the students study places in geography, have them make charts using the five themes of geography as the headings. This will help students understand that the themes are organizational tools used in studying geography.

AT HOME ACTIVITY

- Divide the class into five groups—one group for each of the five themes. Ask students to use newspapers and magazines to find examples in pictures, advertisements, and stories that relate to their theme. Students can assemble their findings in a booklet or poster they can share with the class.

OBJECTIVES

Students will

◆ identify the seven continents, four oceans, North Pole, South Pole, and Equator on a map or globe

◆ identify the Northern, Southern, Eastern, and Western Hemispheres on a map or globe

◆ recognize polar projections

MATERIALS NEEDED

oranges
knife
black and red pens or markers
Transparencies 1, 2
Blackline Masters T34, T35

VOCABULARY

globe	hemisphere
continents	Northern Hemisphere
oceans	Southern Hemisphere
North Pole	Eastern Hemisphere
South Pole	Western Hemisphere
Equator	

INTRODUCING THE SKILL

◆ Help students understand that all places on Earth are located in two hemispheres: the Northern or Southern and the Eastern or Western. Ask students to bring an orange to class. Have them use a black pen or marker to draw a line around the middle of the orange to form a circle. Then have students write the letter *N* (*for Northern*) above the black line, on opposite sides of the orange. Then have them write the letter *S* (*for Southern*) below the black line, directly under each *N* that they have written. Then have students use a red pen or marker to draw another line around the orange, through the top and bottom, between the sides labeled *N* and *S*. Have students write the letter *E* (*for Eastern*) next to the *N* and *S* that are to the right of the red line. Have them write the letter *W* (*for Western*) next to the opposite *N* and *S*. Help students cut the orange along the black line, then along the red line. Show them that each quarter of the orange has two letters written on it. Have students eat the quarters in the following order: NE, SE, NW, SW.

TEACHING NOTES

Page 8 Explain to students that geographers do not always agree on which lines of longitude should be used to separate the Eastern and Western Hemispheres. First, use a globe to show students the Prime Meridian at 0 degrees. Then show them the 180-degree line of longitude. Explain that many geographers use these lines to divide the hemispheres since these lines mark the division between the eastern and western lines of longitude. Then, point out 20°W longitude and 160°E longitude on the globe as you explain that other geographers used these lines to divide the hemispheres. Ask students why they think some geographers divide the hemispheres using these meridians. (*This allows geographers to keep Europe and Africa entirely in the Eastern Hemisphere.*) Use Transparency 1 to review with students.

Page 9 Use Transparency 2 with students. Tell students that the maps shown on this page are polar projections that show how Earth would appear from above the North Pole or from below the South Pole. You may wish to show students a globe from the perspective of the polar projections.

Page 12 After students have completed this page, provide them with copies of the blackline maps of the Eastern and Western Hemispheres on page T34. Have students make a diagram of the four hemispheres similar to the ones on pages 10 and 11. Have them label the Equator, the four hemispheres, the continents, and the oceans. Then have them make a table showing the continents and oceans and the hemispheres in which they are located.

EXTENSION ACTIVITIES

◆ Divide the class into two teams. Have students play "Around the World" using the atlas map of the world on pages 92–93. Ask questions that require students to locate countries and hemispheres. For example, "Which continent in the Eastern Hemisphere is also a country?" (*Australia*) Teams should score one point for each correct answer. The winner is the team that has the most points at the end of a specified time period.

◆ Have students work in groups to research the north and south magnetic poles. Ask them to present the information in a written report.

AT HOME ACTIVITY

◆ Provide students with copies of the blackline map of the world on page T35. Have them color and label the continents and oceans. Then have them cut it apart into continents and oceans to make a puzzle. Have them share their puzzle with younger family members or neighbors to teach them continents and oceans.

OBJECTIVES

Students will
◆ find the purpose of a map by reading the title
◆ read the legend to identify symbols on a map
◆ read the compass rose
◆ determine relative location

MATERIALS NEEDED

compasses
Transparency 3
current newspapers and magazine articles
Blackline Master T35

VOCABULARY

map	compass rose
title	cardinal directions
legend	intermediate directions

INTRODUCING THE SKILL

◆ Provide compasses for students and teach them how to use a compass. Have students work with a partner to determine the cardinal and intermediate directions on the playground. Then allow students to take turns leading the class around the school grounds using their compass. Ask students to name landmarks near the school and their directions relative to the school.

◆ Give students twenty seconds in which to draw a mountain. Have students share their drawings. Discuss the similarities in the drawings. Ask students if they found it easy or difficult to draw a mountain. Then give students twenty seconds to draw a state capital. Share the drawings, and discuss the difficulty of drawing a state capital. Tell students that sometimes cartographers, or mapmakers, are able to use symbols on maps that resemble what they stand for, such as a mountain. But other times, cartographers use dots, stars, colors, or patterns to stand for things on a map.

TEACHING NOTES

Page 14 Use Transparency 3 with students as you work through this page.
Pages 14 and 15 Have students work in pairs to ask each other questions about the relative direction of places shown on these maps. Remind students to refer to the symbols shown in the legend when asking or answering their questions.
Page 17 Explain that Canada is divided into provinces and territories. Point out that each province or territory, like each state in the United States, has a capital city. Call attention to the difference between the symbol for international boundaries and the symbol for provincial or state boundaries used on the map on this page. As students do the first activity on this page, help them follow the international boundary line across the Great Lakes. Explain that cartographers often do not show boundary lines along borders formed by bodies of water. As students do the second activity, point out that the Red River forms the boundary line between North Dakota and Minnesota. Ask students, "What other bodies of water form the boundaries between countries, states, or provinces?" (*Ottawa River, St. Lawrence River, Great Lakes, Columbia River*)
Page 19 Have a volunteer locate the West Indies on a wall map of the world. Then have students describe the location of the West Indies from the following locations: the United States (*southeast*); Central America (*east*); South America (*north*); Africa (*west*); Europe (*southwest*).

EXTENSION ACTIVITIES

◆ Have students collect newspaper and magazine articles about an area or event that is making front-page news. Ask students to locate the area on the atlas map on pages 92–93, then make their own map. Have students track the path of a hurricane, color places that are in conflict, and so on.

◆ Have students make maps with special symbols that correspond to a social studies chapter. For example, students might make maps that show the locations of castles in England, sunken ships in the Atlantic Ocean, well-known architecture throughout the world, major archeological sites in China, or mineral resources in Africa. Students' maps should include a title, legend, and compass rose.

◆ Have students work in pairs to plan an around-the-world cruise. Provide them with copies of the blackline map of the world on page T35. Have them trace the route they would take on the map. If they wish to add islands, they can refer to a more detailed map. Ask students to write journal entries in which they name the direction and the body of water they sailed to get from port to port. Ask them to research at least two of the places they visited on their imaginary trip and use their journal to tell what points of interest they visited.

AT HOME ACTIVITY

◆ Have students listen to a news broadcast with family members and write the names of three places mentioned in the news. Then have them locate the places on a map and write the direction of those places from their home.

Geography Themes Up Close

OBJECTIVES

Students will
◆ describe movement of people, goods, information, and ideas
◆ interpret a map illustrating major transportation networks
◆ interpret a chart
◆ compare communication networks among nations

MATERIALS NEEDED

The World Almanac

VOCABULARY

charts

INTRODUCING THE SKILL

◆ Have students name transportation and communication networks that they or family members use. Discuss with the class the types of networks in their community that are used to move people, goods, information, and ideas. Explain that in this feature, they will learn more about the geography theme of movement.

TEACHING NOTES

Page 20   Read and discuss with students the introductory paragraph on page 20. Call on students to answer the questions in the paragraph. Then have students use the map on page 20 to answer the questions.
◆ Ask students to look at the map of Central America on page 15 of their book. Ask students: What transportation network is shown on the map? (*Pan-American Highway*) What does it connect? (*South America, Central America, and Mexico*) How do the transportation networks in Central America compare to the transportation networks in Russia? (*There is only one major transportation network shown in Central America. Russia has several transportation networks.*)
◆ Have students look at the map of Libya on page 24. Ask: What transportation network is shown on the map on this page? (*Oil pipelines*) Why do these pipelines all go to cities on the Mediterranean Sea? (*The cities on the Mediterranean Sea may have shipping networks that transport the oil to other parts of the world by way of the Mediterranean Sea.*)

◆ Have students look at the map of Northern Africa on page 26. Ask students why they think Tripoli, Libya, is connected with Nguigmi, Niger, by a caravan route. (*Tripoli is located on the Mediterranean Sea so it is probably a trade center. Nguigmi is located in a landlocked country, or a country without a seacoast, so it would need to get goods from a trade center.*)

Page 21   Ask students questions about the chart: What communication tool do most people in Libya have access to? Which country has more newspapers than the United States? Have students make a list of questions to ask about the chart. Call on volunteers to ask their questions.
◆ Have students share their answers to question 6. Point out to students that information such as that shown in the chart is published in statistical abstracts and in almanacs such as *The World Almanac*. Have students find communication information about other countries using these sources.

EXTENSION ACTIVITIES

◆ Have students research the air and sea routes in the world. Have them make maps showing these routes.
◆ Assign students different countries in the world. If possible, help students to find the Internet web pages for these countries. World Wide Web pages for some countries are listed in *The World Almanac*. Ask students to report their findings to the class.
◆ Help students search the Internet for copies of newspapers from other countries. If possible, ask them to print the newspapers. Allow students time to review the newspapers so they can compare and contrast them with newspapers found in the United States.
◆ Have students find other maps that show transportation routes or networks. Ask students to share their findings with the class.

AT HOME ACTIVITY

◆ Have students work with family members to collect labels from goods. Ask them to read the labels to determine where the goods originated. Then display the labels around the borders of a large world map on the bulletin board. Use yarn or ribbons to connect each label to its country of origin.

③ Scale and Distance

OBJECTIVES

Students will
- use a map scale to determine distances in miles and kilometers
- compare scales on inset maps with scales on larger maps
- understand the relationship of the map scale to actual size

MATERIALS NEEDED

scale models: airplanes, cars, trains, houses
globe
ruler or string
Transparency 4
Blackline Master T26
art materials: paper towel tubes, Styrofoam, coat hangers

VOCABULARY

map scale   kilometers
miles   inset map

INTRODUCING THE SKILL

◆ Have students bring to class scale models they have made, such as airplanes, dollhouses, cars, and trains. Discuss how these models are miniature representations of real things. Ask students what scales were used to construct each model. Then show students a globe. Ask students how globes are scale models or Earth. Explain to students that in Chapter 3 they will learn how maps are drawn to scale.

◆ Review with students different ways to determine distance on a map by using a ruler, a piece of paper, or a piece of string. Pair students who have difficulty measuring distances with those who have mastered the skill. Assign problems for students to practice measuring distances on different maps.

TEACHING NOTES

Page 22   Use Transparency 4 with students as they study the map of Africa. Ask students to find the distance in miles between pairs of cities shown on the map.

Page 23   Divide the class into cooperative learning groups. For additional practice with map skills, provide students with copies of the **Map Attack!** blackline on page T26. Have them complete numbers 1–5 and 9 using maps from their basal text.

Page 24   Before using this page, have students look at the map of Africa on page 22. Ask them to locate Tripoli. Tell them that Tripoli is the capital of Libya. Now direct students' attention to the map on page 24. Point out that this map is also a map of Libya. Explain that oil is an important industry in Libya. Oil accounts for almost all of the country's export earnings. Mention that Libya is a member of the Organization of Petroleum Exporting Countries (OPEC). Then have students draw an oil pipeline from oil field #2 to Hofra. Ask them to measure the length of this pipeline. (*about 140 MI or about 230 KM*)

Page 25   You may wish to have students use string to measure the distances of rivers that curve.

Page 26   Have students work in pairs to make up story problems, such as the one used for item number 6 on this page. Then have students exchange and solve each other's story problems.

EXTENSION ACTIVITIES

◆ Have students do research to find out more about the metric system of measurement and the English system of measurement. Ask them to identify some of the countries that use each system.

◆ Have an architect or construction supervisor talk to the class about blueprints and the use of scale in their jobs. Have students prepare questions before the discussion.

◆ Have students construct large-scale models of familiar objects, such as a pencil, an eraser, or a paper clip. Have them measure the item, then multiply that number by ten. Gather paper towel tubes, Styrofoam, and coat hangers. Have students construct the oversized objects. Ask them to make labels indicating the scale they used.

◆ Have students make inset maps for the map on page 26. Allow students to choose from the area of Africa that interests them. Maps should include a compass rose, title, and map scale. Display the inset maps.

◆ Divide the class into five groups to research and construct a scale model of the following canals: Suez Canal, Panama Canal, Erie Canal, Kiel Canal and the Corinth Canal. Ask each group to write a short report describing the location of the canal, its length, width, and depth, the number of locks, the date it opened, the amount of tonnage carried through the canal each year, and other interesting facts about the canal.

AT HOME ACTIVITY

◆ Have students work with a family member to measure each room in their home. Have students determine scale and use the measurements to draw a map of their home. Have them label each room and include a map scale on their map.

OBJECTIVES

Students will
- read and interpret symbols on a route map
- recognize junctions and interchanges
- recognize and use mileage markers
- use a map index and a grid

MATERIALS NEEDED

various road maps
The Travels of Marco Polo, edited by William Marsden
map of Marco Polo's route
Transparency 5
Blackline Masters T26, T27–T33 or T35, T28 and T29

VOCABULARY

junction	grid
interchange	coordinate
mileage markers	map index

INTRODUCING THE SKILL

- Give students the opportunity to look at various road maps. Ask students to name one thing that road maps show. Write their responses on the chalkboard. Then ask students to describe the useful purposes of road maps. (*finding the directions and distances to places, planning road trips, estimating the time it will take to drive to a place, giving information about things to see and do*)
- Read to students excerpts from *The Travels of Marco Polo,* edited by William Marsden, that describe Polo's travels from Venice, Italy, to China and other places in Asia during the mid-1200s. Show students Marco Polo's route on a wall map of the world. (*Marco Polo's route can be found in* The World Book Encyclopedia.) Discuss with students how Marco Polo knew which way to go on his travels. Then tell students that in Chapter 4 they will learn how to read route maps.

TEACHING NOTES

Page 28 Use Transparency 5 with students as you work with the route map and introduce the vocabulary on this page. Have students identify and distinguish between the different kinds of highways shown on the map.

Page 29 Explain to students that they can use a map index to help them locate places on a map. Point out to students that the numbers circled on the map can also be found in the index. Have students plan a walking tour of central New Orleans. Tell them that their time is limited, so they can only visit six places that interest them. Have students draw a route from one place on their tour to the next. Then have them write the streets and the cardinal or intermediate directions they would take to get from place to place and the coordinates of each place visited.

Page 30 Have students work in pairs to make road signs such as the one shown in number 7. Have students exchange their signs with other pairs and determine in which city or town they would see the sign.

Page 31 Ask students to circle the following points of interest in Toronto as they name the coordinates: Marine Museum (*F-2*), Old Fort York (*F-2*), Union Station (*E-3*), City Hall (*E-3*), Zoo (*D-4*), and Ontario Science Center (*A-5*).

Page 32 Ask students to look at the map scale on the map of Southern Quebec. Ask students why the map scale shows only kilometers? (*Canada uses the metric system of measurement.*)

Page 33 For additional review of maps, provide students with copies of the **Map Attack!** blackline on page T26 to use with the map on this page.

EXTENSION ACTIVITIES

- Ask the Chamber of Commerce in your area for road maps of your state. Divide the class into cooperative learning groups. Ask students questions that require them to use the map index and grid, mileage markers, and highway and interchange designations on the state maps.
- Have a truck driver, airline pilot, or railroad engineer talk to the class about the transportation routes they use in their jobs. Have students prepare questions to ask before the discussion.
- Provide copies of copies of the blackline maps on pages T27–T33 or T35. Have students work in small groups to find examples of different kinds of route maps (railroads, ships, airlines, and trade routes in the United States and in other countries). Have students in each group draw and label some of the routes on the blackline maps.
- Provide students with copies of the blackline maps of North America and South America on pages T28 and T29. Have students work with a partner to find the route of the Pan American Highway and draw it on these two maps. Students should label the countries and major cities that the highway connects. Have students tape the two maps together to show the entire highway system.

AT HOME ACTIVITY

- Have students read a local road map and explain to a family member how to get from their home to a place of interest in their community. Students can use the map of their community in the phone book or ask the chamber of commerce for a map of their area.

Geography Themes Up Close

OBJECTIVES

Students will
◆ describe physical features of places using maps
◆ describe human features of places using maps
◆ use maps to determine relationships of human features within a place and among places

INTRODUCING THE SKILL

◆ Make sure students understand the distinction between physical features and human features. Explain that physical features are the natural features of a place that are part of the environment—climate, soil, landforms, bodies of water, and plants and animals. Human features are those created or developed by people that make up their culture, such as art and architecture, types of government, religions, ways of making a living, languages, and so on. Then, have students describe things in their town or city that makes it different from any other place. Write the descriptions on the chalkboard for later use. Explain that in this feature, they will learn more about the things that make places unique.

TEACHING NOTES

Page 34   Read and discuss with students the introductory paragraph on page 34. Call on students to categorize the descriptions of their town or city that were saved on the chalkboard as physical or human features. Ask students if they can add any physical or human features to the list.
◆ After students complete page 34, call on volunteers to share their answers. Point out that the physical and human features of Tokyo mentioned in their answers describe the place known as Tokyo, Japan.
◆ Have students look at the map of Libya on page 24. Ask: What are some physical and human features of Libya? (*Location on the Gulf of Sidra and Mediterranean Sea, cities, oil fields and pipelines, roads*)
◆ Have students look at the map of central New Orleans on page 29. Ask: What is the major physical feature of New Orleans? (*Mississippi River*) Have students use the map index to describe some features people travel to New Orleans to see. (*Entertainment such as museums and theaters*)

Page 35   Have students complete page 35. Then ask them to compare the maps of Tokyo and Paris and discuss the similarities of the two places. (*They both have a river, they both have libraries, parks, gardens, and universities.*) Point out to students that although some of the features in both cities are similar, each place is different from any other place on Earth. On a world map, have students locate Tokyo, Japan, and Paris, France. Discuss how their locations make them unique.

EXTENSION ACTIVITIES

◆ Provide students with brochures from travel agencies showing tours of places. Ask students to use the brochures to make posters of places showing their physical and human features. Display the posters in the classroom.
◆ Assign students to research different countries in the world. Have them write reports about the countries describing the human and physical features of the countries. Their reports should include information about physical features such as climate, landforms, bodies of water, plant and animal life, and soil of the country. They should also include information about the human features such as buildings, universities, customs, and populations. Their reports should include a map showing some features of the country. Have students share their reports with the class.
◆ Remind students that Tokyo and Paris are national capitals. Have students compare and contrast the physical and human features of Tokyo and Paris with the physical and human features of the national capital of the United States, Washington, D.C. Students might organize their findings in a Venn diagram. Interested students might want to compare other national capitals. Then have students write a generalization about the similarities and differences of places that are national capitals.

AT HOME ACTIVITY

◆ Have students work with family members to create a list of physical and human features of their neighborhood. Then have them create a list of physical and human features of their home. Ask volunteers to share their lists with the class.

OBJECTIVES

Students will
◆ read and interpret a relief map
◆ identify features on a relief map
◆ read and interpret an elevation map

MATERIALS NEEDED

Transparency 6
land use map of Afghanistan
Blackline Master T35
books by Sir Edmund P. Hillary

VOCABULARY

relief map	tributaries
source	elevation
mouth	

INTRODUCING THE SKILL

◆ Invite a geologist and/or a cartographer to speak to the class. Have the geologist discuss the importance of studying mountains, and/or have the cartographer discuss how mountains are measured. Have students prepare questions before the presentations. If it is not possible to arrange for these speakers, assign groups of students the roles of geologists and cartographers. Ask them to do research to find out about mountains. Then have them give an oral presentation to the class.
◆ Have students write letters requesting information about mountain climbing to the American Alpine Club, 710 Tenth Street, Suite 100, Golden, CO 80401. Ask volunteers to share their letters and the information they receive.

TEACHING NOTES

Page 36 Use Transparency 6 with students to introduce the concepts on this page.
Pages 36 and 37 Have students compare the maps on pages 36 and 37. Ask: Which map gives a more precise description of the height of the land? (*elevation map*) Which map would you use to find the height of the land in the West Siberian Plain? (*elevation map*) Which map would you use to learn the exact height of Mt. Pobeda? (*relief map*) Which map would you use to find the highest mountain ranges? (*elevation map*)
Page 38 Ask students to name the mountains and rivers in Africa, the direction the rivers flow, and the body of water into which each river empties. (*Atlas Mountains and Ruwenzori; Congo River flows southwest into the Atlantic Ocean; Nile River flows north into the Mediterranean Sea*)
Page 39 Ask students to brainstorm reasons why people would need to know the elevation of the land. Write their responses on the chalkboard.

Page 40 Ask students to make a table showing the elevations of the cities in Turkey.
Page 41 Ask students to predict how the land is used in Afghanistan based on elevation. Write their predictions on the chalkboard. Then have students work in groups to study a land use map of Afghanistan. Ask students to compare the actual land use with their predictions.

EXTENSION ACTIVITIES

◆ Ask students to make a table comparing the elevations of the source and the mouth of several rivers shown on the maps in Chapter 5. Ask students to form a conclusion about elevation and the flow of rivers. (*A river always flows from higher to lower elevation.*)
◆ Have students work with a partner to use an almanac or other sources to make a chart showing the places of highest and lowest elevation and the longest river on each continent.
◆ Provide students with copies of the blackline map of the world on page T35. Ask them to work in pairs using atlas maps to add relief shading to their map to show the following mountain ranges: Rocky Mountains, Appalachian Mountains, Andes, Pyrenees, Atlas, Ural Mountains, The Himalaya, and the Great Dividing Range. Also have students draw and label the following rivers, their sources, and their mouths: Nile, Amazon, Yangtze, Congo, Volga, Mississippi, Tigris, and Danube.
◆ Have students use an almanac or other source to find the mountain range, country of location, elevation, and interesting facts for each of the following mountains: Aconcagua, Annapurna I, Chimborazo, Kanchenjunga, and Godwin Austen (K2). Ask students to present this information in a chart and make a bar graph showing elevations.
◆ Have students make a bar graph showing the heights of the mountain peaks labeled on the maps in Chapter 5.
◆ Have students read one of the books by Sir Edmund P. Hillary about his mountain climbing adventures. *High Adventure* is an account of Hillary's 1953 climb up part of Mt. Everest. *High in the Thin Cold Air* is about the Abominable Snowman. Ask volunteers to dramatize parts of these books for the class.

AT HOME ACTIVITY

◆ Have students work with a family member to make a relief map showing the physical features of an ocean floor. Encyclopedias and books about oceans have maps that show these features.

OBJECTIVES

Students will
- locate specific lines of latitude and longitude on a map or globe
- use latitude and longitude coordinates to locate places

MATERIALS NEEDED

current newspapers and magazine articles
world map, bulletin board, tacks, yarn
Transparency 7
hurricane tracking charts
game: *Where in the World is Carmen Sandiego?*
Blackline Master T35

VOCABULARY

latitude	degrees
longitude	meridians
parallels	Prime Meridian

INTRODUCING THE SKILL

- Review mnemonic devices with your students to help them remember the difference between latitude and longitude. Compare the beginning sound of the word *latitude* with the word *ladder*, or rhyme "lat" (for *latitude*) with "flat." The lines of latitude are like the rungs of a ladder leading up or down a map or globe. Tell students that when they say *longitude* they should think of the vertical, <u>long</u> lines on a map or globe.
- Have students clip and bring to class newspaper articles about current events. Then on a world map, help students locate the places where the events have occurred. Make a bulletin board using the map of the world and the newspaper articles. Use tacks and yarn to connect the newspaper articles and the locations of the places on the map. You might also want to have students use atlases to find the coordinates of the places.

TEACHING NOTES

Page 42   Ask students why they think all lines of latitude and lines of longitude are not drawn and labeled on this map. (*It would be confusing since the lines would be so crowded.*) Remind students that they must estimate the latitude and longitude of a place if the place does not lie on any of the lines that are drawn or labeled on a map or globe. Then use Transparency 7 with students and have them practice estimating the latitude and longitude of the cities shown on this map.

Page 43   Have students work with partners to estimate the coordinates of other places on the map on this page.

Page 44   Divide the class into cooperative learning groups. Provide a globe for each group. Have students locate the Prime Meridian at 0°. Point out that the number of degrees increases on the lines of longitude to the east and west of the Prime Meridian. Ask students to name the highest numbered line of longitude. (*180°*) Point out that, like the Prime Meridian, the 180° line of longitude is neither <u>east</u> nor <u>west</u>. Ask students why this is so. (*because there is only one and it is the dividing line*) Next, demonstrate the importance of labeling coordinates N, S, E, or W. Ask students to name the continent located at 160° longitude. (*North America and Asia.*) Then ask: What continent is located at 160°W longitude? (*North America*) What continent is located 160°E longitude? (*Asia*) Ask students to explain why this map is not a world map. (*Asia, Australia, Antarctica, and the Indian Ocean are not shown.*) Have students note that the degrees are labeled every 20° but that the in-between 10° lines are shown for reference.

Page 45   Ask students to identify the hemisphere shown on this map. (*Eastern*) Next, have students add and label the following cities on the map using these rounded-off coordinates: Johannesburg (*25°S, 30°E*); Oslo (*60°N, 10°E*); Kuala Lumpur (*5°N, 100°E*); Norlisk (*70°N, 90°E*); Perth (*30°S, 115°E*).

Page 46   Have students plot the path of other hurricanes. You can obtain hurricane tracking charts and coordinates from the National Weather Service (or perhaps your local weather service).

Page 47   Give students additional practice using latitude and longitude by having them use textbook or atlas maps of the United States or the Western Hemisphere. Ask them to estimate the latitude and longitude of the following cities: Honolulu, Hawaii (*20°N, 160°W*); Barrow, Alaska (*70°N, 155°W*); Juneau, Alaska (*60°N, 135°W*).

EXTENSION ACTIVITIES

- Have students work in groups to create a board game using latitude and longitude. Have groups explain their game to the class. Give students time to play each other's games.
- Allow students time to play the computer game, *Where in the World is Carmen Sandiego?* Have them work in pairs or in small groups. Have students use a world map to estimate the latitude and longitude coordinates of the places where they track down the international thieves.

AT HOME ACTIVITY

- Provide students with copies of the blackline map of the world on page T35. Ask students to work with a family member to track the travels of their favorite sports team, music group, or political figure.

OBJECTIVES

Students will
◆ identify relative locations on maps and globes
◆ relate the location of places relative to physical features
◆ label locations on a map
◆ identify absolute locations of places on maps using latitude and longitude coordinates

VOCABULARY

location
absolute location
relative location

INTRODUCING THE SKILL

◆ Discuss with students the importance of knowing the locations of places.
◆ Ask students to describe their location in the classroom. As students describe their locations, write on the chalkboard the descriptive words and phrases the students use to describe their locations in the classroom. These words and phrases might include *near, close to, next to, behind, in front of,* and *surrounded by.* Explain that these types of words and phrases describe the <u>relative</u> location of students in relation to other people or things in the classroom. Students may also use other descriptive words and phrases to describe their location in the classroom including *fourth seat in the fifth row, first chair at the second table,* and *third person in the last row.* Explain that these types of words and phrases describe the <u>actual</u>, or absolute, location of students in the classroom. Point out that in this feature students will learn about the relative and absolute locations of places.

TEACHING NOTES

Page 48 Have students read the introductory paragraph on this page. Ask: When would it be helpful to know the relative location of a place? (*to give someone directions to a place*) When would it be necessary to know the absolute location of a place? (*to give the exact address or actual latitude and longitude coordinates of a place*).
◆ Have students look at the pictures of globes on pages 8 and 9 of their books. Ask students: In which hemispheres is South America located? (*Western Hemisphere and both the Northern Hemisphere and the Southern Hemisphere*) How would you describe the location of South America

relative to the Equator? (*A small part of northern South America is north of the Equator, but most of South America is south of the Equator.*)
◆ Ask students to look at the map of the world on pages 92 and 93 in the atlas of their book. What is the location of South America relative to the other continents? (*South America is south of North America, west of Africa, southwest of Europe, north of Antarctica, west of Australia, and southwest of Asia.*)
Page 49 Have students share their answers to questions 6 and 10 on this page. Discuss the fact that there are many ways of describing the relative location of a place. Also explain that the absolute location of a landform is usually given as the latitude and longitude coordinates near the center or middle of the landform. Have students practice this by using the map to determine the absolute locations of the following South American countries: Venezuela ($6°N$, $65°W$), Guyana ($5°N$, $58°W$), Suriname ($4°N$, $55°W$), French Guiana ($4°N$, $53°W$), Colombia ($4°N$, $73°W$), Brazil ($11°S$, $54°W$), Ecuador ($2°S$, $78°W$), Peru ($9°S$, $75°W$), Bolivia ($15°S$, $65°W$), Paraguay ($23 1/2°S$ [Tropic of Capricorn], $56°W$), Chile ($33°S$, $71°W$) and Argentina ($37°S$, $65°W$). Then, ask students to use the map to give the absolute locations of the following cities: Quito ($0°$, $78°W$), Caracas ($10°N$, $67°W$), Georgetown ($7°N$, $58°W$), and Buenos Aires ($34°S$, $58°W$).

EXTENSION ACTIVITIES

◆ Have students compare and contrast the locations of major cities in South America with the locations of major cities in Europe and Asia. Ask them to note the geographic factors that may have influenced the locations of the cities.
◆ Have students work in small groups to write two questions about location using the information in the map on page 48. Then have each group ask the rest of the class their questions.

AT HOME ACTIVITY

◆ Have students work with family members to determine the region(s) or country(ies) from which their ancestors came. Ask them to describe the location of these region(s) or country(ies) in relation to the where the students and their family members live today. Also, ask them to determine the absolute locations of the region(s) or country(ies) from which their ancestors came.

OBJECTIVES

Students will

◆ read a climate map
◆ identify areas of the world as being in the Torrid Zone, Frigid Zone, and Temperate Zones
◆ identify the unique characteristics of the Torrid Zone, Frigid Zones, and Temperate Zones
◆ identify other factors that affect climate

MATERIALS NEEDED

Transparency 8
flashlight and globe
Blackline Masters T34, T28
newspaper weather map

VOCABULARY

climate	middle latitudes
climate zones	Temperate Zones
low latitudes	high latitudes
Torrid Zone	Frigid Zones

INTRODUCING THE SKILL

◆ Ask students to explain the difference between the terms *climate* and *weather*. (Climate *is the pattern of weather a certain place has over a long period of time.* Weather *is the condition of Earth's atmosphere at a certain place and time.*) Next, have the students write descriptions of the climate and today's weather for their community.

◆ Have students brainstorm different aspects of climate that can be shown on a map. Have them find examples of climate maps in atlases, geography textbooks, newspapers, and magazines. Ask students to share their climate maps with the class.

TEACHING NOTES

Page 50 Use Transparency 8 to introduce the climate zones to students. After teaching page 50, use a flashlight and a globe to show that the low altitudes receive the sun's most direct rays and the middle and high latitudes receive indirect rays.

Page 51 Point out to students that, in order to make it easier to study Earth, geographers divide the world into regions. One way they divide Earth is into climate regions. Ask students to name other types of regions geographers use to divide Earth. (*political regions, landform regions, language regions, religious regions, vegetation regions, and so on*)

Page 52 Provide students with copies of the blackline maps of the Eastern and Western Hemispheres on page T34. Have them make maps showing the high, middle, and low latitudes. Have them label the Torrid Zone, Frigid Zones, and Temperate Zones.

Page 53 Remind students that although two places might be located at the same latitude, they may have different climates. Divide the class into small groups. Have students use world political maps to locate cities at approximately the same latitudes as the cities shown on the map. Then have students determine the climate zones of the cities. Challenge students to think of reasons why places in the same latitudes are in different climate zones. (*altitude, proximity to water*)

Page 54 Tell students to plan a trip to Europe to four cities in four different climate zones. Have students name each city, its climate zone, and the direction they travel from one place to another. Have them list clothes to take for each city.

EXTENSION ACTIVITIES

◆ Have students look up climatic information for their own region or state. Ask them to make graphs or tables to present average monthly temperatures, annual precipitation, and number of days of sunshine. Ask students to write conclusions they can make from the information.

◆ Invite a meteorologist to class to explain these terms: *cold fronts, warm fronts, barometric pressure, humidity, wind chill factor, dew point,* and so on, as well as weather map symbols. Have students prepare questions before the discussion. Afterwards, have students create weather maps by using the blackline map of North America on page T28.

◆ Have students work in small groups to research and then draw a diagram to show why it is summer in the Southern Hemisphere when it is winter in the Northern Hemisphere. (*Southern Hemisphere points more directly toward the sun and receives more direct, and hotter, rays from the sun, while the Northern Hemisphere tilts away from the sun and receives less direct rays.*)

◆ Have students work in pairs to research various weather conditions: hurricanes, tornadoes, cyclones, thunderstorms, and so on. Have students learn how and why these conditions occur.

◆ Divide the class into three groups. Assign each group one of the following factors to research and explain how it affects climate: elevation, wind and ocean currents, and landforms. Have each group present their findings using graphs, tables, pictures, flow charts, or diagrams.

AT HOME ACTIVITY

◆ Have students use a weather map from a daily newspaper or a weather report on the television news to help them give a "weather report" to family members. Students might want to make weather maps to use for their "weather report."

8 Combining Maps

OBJECTIVES

Students will
- read a map that combines several kinds of information
- draw conclusions about the relationship between facts on a combined map

MATERIALS NEEDED

Transparency 9
blank overhead transparencies
Blackline Master T27, T35

VOCABULARY

relationships
population density

INTRODUCING THE SKILL

◆ Have students brainstorm a list of the kinds of information that can be shown on a map. Write the list on chart paper, and hang it on the wall. Then have students bring to class maps that combine at least two sets of facts. Discuss the information shown on the maps. Ask students if the types of information shown on the maps are the same as the types of information listed on the chart.

◆ Divide the class into two groups. Ask one group to draw a mural-size map of the school grounds. Ask the other group to draw a mural-size map of the inside of the school. Then help the two groups tape their maps together. Ask students how the combined map enhances their knowledge of the school. Then tell students that in Chapter 8 they will learn how combining maps helps them draw conclusions based on different kinds of information.

TEACHING NOTES

Page 56 Use Transparency 9 with students to introduce the information on this page.

Pages 56 and 57 Divide the class into small groups. Help students use the information shown on the maps on pages 56 and 57 to make a table describing the following information about the cities on these maps: climate, physical features, population density. You may wish to use the chalkboard to make a sample table for one of the cities shown on these maps.

Pages 58 and 59 Have students work in small groups to make a list of generalizations from conclusions they draw about the information shown on the maps on pages 58 and 59. Have one student from each group record the group's conclusions. Then have another student report the generalizations to the class.

Page 60 Have students continue reading the combined map on this page by asking additional questions. Examples: What information is combined on this map? (*areas of poor farming, population density, relief*) At about what degree of latitude north and south of the Equator does the land become too cold for farming? (*at about 60°*) Which of these areas of poor farming has the highest population density? (*the area labeled "too dry for farming"*) What do you think the light green areas on the map represent? (*areas suitable for farming*)

Page 61 Ask students to identify the information combined on this map. (*political divisions of Australia, climate, relief*) Have students compare this map of Australia with the map on page 56.

EXTENSION ACTIVITIES

◆ Divide the class into small groups. Provide each group with a blank overhead transparency and a copy of the blackline map of the United States on page T27. Ask students to trace the blackline map on the transparency. Have students show one type of information for the United States on their transparency. (*Examples: political, relief, climate, population density, land use, natural resources, agricultural products, manufacturing products, and transportation routes*) Then use the overhead projector to combine the maps by overlapping two or more of students' transparencies. Have students draw conclusions about the relationship of facts on the overlapped maps.

◆ Provide students with copies of the blackline map of the world on page T35. Have students make maps combining major ocean trade routes and ocean currents. Discuss the relationship of the ocean currents and the trade routes.

◆ Have students make a table of information about European cities using the information shown on the maps on pages 58 and 59. Students should use the following headings in their table: climate, physical features, population density. Have students use this information to decide in which ten European cities they would most like to live. Discuss students' lists and the reasons for their choices.

AT HOME ACTIVITIES

◆ Have students work with a family member to make a map of their neighborhood. The maps should show streets, homes or apartments, and important landmarks. Then have students discuss with a family member one other fact they would like to include in the map. For example, the map might show population density of the homes or apartments in the neighborhood, trees in the neighborhood, homes with cable television, homes with basketball hoops, homes with dogs, and so on. All maps should include a map title, legend, and compass rose.

Geography Themes Up Close

OBJECTIVES

Students will
◆ describe ways people interact with their environment
◆ interpret maps showing the impact of human interaction on the environment
◆ define terms which describe the impact of technology upon the environment

VOCABULARY

desertification
reclaim
polders

INTRODUCING THE SKILL

◆ Have students individually brainstorm a list of ways in which people depend upon the environment. After a few minutes, ask students to share their lists with the class. Explain that in this feature they will learn how humans affect the environment and the environment affects humans.
◆ Have students find pictures in newspapers and magazines of ways that people adapt to the environment. Create a collage using the pictures.

TEACHING NOTES

Page 62   Read and discuss with students the introductory paragraph on page 62. Explain to students that certain factors contribute to desertification. Climate changes and droughts can cause deserts to expand. Humans also contribute to desertification. Fertile land is lost due to the overgrazing of animals. This causes a loss of plant life. Without the protective cover of plants, wind and water increase soil erosion. Other contributing factors include poor farming methods, such as cutting down too many trees. Create a chart on the chalkboard using the following headings: Environment Affects People, and People Affect the Environment. Call on volunteers to help complete the chart with examples for each heading.
◆ Discuss with students the impact of the growth of the desert in North Africa. Ask: How does desertification affect the people who live in North Africa? (*The people in North Africa are left with less area that can be used for farming and grazing. Therefore, people are losing their ways of life.*) What can be done to help stop desertification? (*Trees and plants can be replanted and irrigation could be used to provide water. People could move their herds before the grasses and plants have been eaten to the roots.*)
◆ Have students look at the map of Areas of Poor Farming in the World on page 60. Have students explain how this map shows an effect of the environment on people. (*Places that are either too dry, too cold, or too rough for farming have fewer people than areas that are good for farming.*) What parts of Africa are suitable for farming? (*most of Africa south of the Sahara*) What parts of the United States are good for farming? (*all except parts of the southwest and the Rocky Mountain region*)
◆ Point out to students that the maps on pages 56 and 57 and on pages 58 and 59 illustrate the effect of the environment on people. Have students work in small groups to analyze the maps and draw conclusions about the effect of climate on populations.

Page 63   Inform students that IJsselmeer is a lake. Also, point out to students the difference between the national capital (*Amsterdam*) and its symbol, and the provincial capital (*The Hague*) and its symbol on the map and in the legend.
◆ Have students read the paragraph and then use the map to answer the questions on page 63. Discuss answers with students, especially to the last question. Point out to students that anytime the environment is altered, there can be changes to the environment. These changes sometimes, but not always, cause harm to the environment. Ask students what possible effects can happen as a result of draining the water to create polders. (*Plant and animal life that depended on the water could probably die.*)

EXTENSION ACTIVITIES

◆ Have students research, using current magazine and newspaper articles and the Internet, to examine the impact of technology on the rain forests of the world. If possible, have students make maps showing the extent of the rain forests 25 years ago and the extent of the rain forests today. Also, have students write brief reports explaining the human/environment interactions that have led to the loss of rain forests.
◆ Have students look in newspapers and magazines to find pictures and maps that show how people have changed the environment. Create a bulletin board to show these examples.
◆ Ask students to sketch various methods of land use, such as irrigation in dry areas, terraces on hilly areas, flood control, and mining. Display the sketches.

AT HOME ACTIVITY

◆ Have students work with family members to analyze how their family affects or adapts to the environment. Ask them to analyze whether the impact on the environment is positive or negative. Have them brainstorm ways to be more environmentally friendly.

OBJECTIVES

Students will
◆ compare two maps with different information about the same country or region
◆ draw conclusions based on maps

MATERIALS NEEDED

various maps of your state
Transparency 10
Blackline Master T35, T31
vegetation map of the world

VOCABULARY

comparing

INTRODUCING THE SKILL

◆ Have students compare two maps of their state that present different types of information. First, have students examine one map and tell what information each map presents. Ask students questions that require them to compare the maps. For example, if students are looking at a natural resource map and an agricultural map, ask them to name the part(s) of their state where a specific crop and mineral can be found. Tell students that in Chapter 9 they will learn how to compare two maps that give different information about the same country or region.

TEACHING NOTES

Page 64　Use Transparency 10 with students as you work the exercises on this page.
Page 66　Call students' attention to the symbol in the legend that indicates principal crops. Explain to students that any symbol shown in the legend can appear in red to indicate that it is a principal crop.
Page 67　Point out that any symbol in this legend can appear in red to indicate that it is a principal mineral. Explain to students that in order to answer some of the questions on this page they must compare the map on this page with the map on page 66. Then have students use both maps to create a table showing the following information about countries in Europe: land use, agricultural products, manufacturing centers, and mineral resources.
Page 68　Ask students additional questions to give them more practice with drawing conclusions about the information shown on the maps on this page. Examples: How much precipitation do grapes require to grow? (*less than 100 centimeters*) Near what physical features are goats and sheep generally raised? (*hills and mountains*)

Page 69　Have students work in small groups and use atlases and encyclopedias to find other maps of Japan, such as precipitation maps and relief maps, to compare with the maps on this page. Each group should write five questions that compare the maps. Have a recorder in each group write the questions. Then have groups exchange maps and answer another group's questions.

EXTENSION ACTIVITIES

◆ Divide the class into cooperative learning groups. Have students make an atlas of four or five maps of the country of their choice. They should include some of the following maps in their atlas: physical, precipitation, population, climate, crop, and resource maps. Afterwards, have them compare the maps and write ten conclusions they can draw from the information shown on the maps.
◆ Divide the class into groups. Have students use an encyclopedia or other reference book to locate information about India's imports and exports. Provide them copies of the blackline map of the world on page T35. Have them show products that are imported to India (by drawing arrows from products in other countries to India) and products that are exported from India to other countries (by drawing arrows from products in India to other countries). The maps should indicate India's main trading partners and include a legend.
◆ Divide the class into two groups. Provide students with copies of the blackline map of Africa on page T31. Ask one group to research and draw a historical map showing European Colonial Rule in Africa in 1914. Ask the other group to label and color the present-day political map of Africa. Then have students work in pairs to compare the two maps. Have students draw conclusions based on the maps. Ask students to brainstorm a list of other maps of Africa that they would find interesting to compare with these maps.
◆ Have students compare a vegetation map of the world with the climate map of the world on page 53. Then have them make tables showing climate zones and the kinds of vegetation found in them. Ask students to write generalizations about the kinds of vegetation grown in each climate zone.

AT HOME ACTIVITY

◆ Have students work with a family member to compare early land use maps with present-day land use maps of their community. Community land use maps should be available through the library, local government, chamber of commerce, or state government. Have students write a paragraph describing any changes in land use.

OBJECTIVES

Students will
- explain why there are 24 time zones
- determine the time in a specific place, given the time in another time zone
- explain the function of the International Date Line

MATERIALS NEEDED

Transparency 11
globe and flashlight
several clocks
brads

VOCABULARY

standard time zones
International Date Line

INTRODUCING THE SKILL

- Have students brainstorm a list of reasons they might need to know the time in another time zone. (*traveling, sporting events, TV programming, making long distance phone calls, and so on*) Write the list on the chalkboard.
- Review A.M. and P.M. with students. Tell them the following mnemonic devices: A.M. is "After Midnight," and P.M. is "Preparing for Midnight."

TEACHING NOTES

Page 70   Use Transparency 11 with students as you study this page. Then, help students get a better idea of how the sun and Earth's rotation affect the time of day on Earth. Use a globe and a flashlight. Shine the flashlight on one side of the globe. Ask students how much of the globe is in the light and how much of the globe is in darkness. Then, slowly turn the globe toward the east. Ask students if the same parts of the globe are always in the light. Ask students to explain how this activity shows time changes on Earth.

Page 71   Point out to students that time zones are based on degrees of longitude. Ask students to compute the number of degrees of longitude in each time zone based on the following facts: There are 360 lines of longitude on the globe. There are 24 time zones. (*360 degrees ÷ 24 time zones = 15 degrees per time zone*)

Page 72   Reinforce the concept that when students travel east the time will be later, so they will have to set their watch ahead one hour for each time zone they cross. When they travel west, the time will be earlier, and they will set their watch back one hour for each time zone they cross. Have students practice using time zones by answering questions about the map on this page.

Page 74   Have students make a chart similar to the one on this page, but have them replace London with Washington, D.C., as their departure location.

Page 75   Ask students to identify the time zone in which your community is located. Then have them work in pairs to write story problems similar to number 5 on this page. Have pairs exchange story problems and complete the answers.

EXTENSION ACTIVITIES

- Bring several clocks into the classroom. Line them up under a large map of the world. Label each clock with a different place around the world, such as London, New York City, San Francisco, and Tokyo. Have students help you calculate the time in each city. Set each clock with the appropriate time. Periodically throughout the day, ask students to determine what time and what day it is in each place. Discuss what people in those locations would be doing.
- Ask students to pretend that they have a business in Hawaii. They must make frequent phone calls and plane trips to Sydney, Australia (*an eight-hour flight*). Have students keep a log of what time and day phone calls were made in Hawaii and when they were received in Sydney. Students should also plan a business trip and tell the day and time of their departure from Hawaii and the day and time of their arrival in Sydney. Remind students to take the International Date Line in to consideration.
- Have students make their own "Time Zone Dial" of the Northern Hemisphere. Have them cut out the rectangle that contains the drawing on page 71. Next, have them cut out the circle that forms the Northern Hemisphere and glue it to a piece of cardboard the same size. (The times and arrows should remain on the rectangle.) Then, have them glue the rest of the rectangle to a whole piece of cardboard the same size. Finally, have them attach the Northern Hemisphere back in its original place on the rectangle with a brad in the middle. The brad allows movement between the circle and the rectangle. Students can use this dial to figure the time in all Northern Hemisphere time zones by moving the circle to the right or to the left.
- Have students work in small groups. Assign each group one of the following aspects of time to research: midnight sun, circadian rhythms, relative motion. Have each group explain the information they obtain.

AT HOME ACTIVITY

- Have students work with a family member to construct a sundial. Have them keep a chart to record the accuracy of the sundial at various times during a week.

Carta a las Familias

Fecha _____

Estimada familia:

A lo largo de este año escolar, su hijo o hija aprenderá y practicará destrezas de geografía usando *Maps•Globes•Graphs, Level F*. En los doce capítulos, su hijo o hija aprenderá a identificar los continentes, océanos, polos Norte y Sur, el Ecuador y los hemisferios en un mapa y en el globo terráqueo. Su hijo o hija también trabajará con claves de mapas, direcciones, escala y distancia y latitud y longitud para interpretar diferentes tipos de mapas. Algunos de éstos incluyen mapas de relieve y elevación, mapas de clima y mapas que combinan diferentes tipos de información. Su hijo o hija también estudiará el huso horario y proyecciones polares y llegará a comprender y crear varios tipos de gráficas y tablas.

Usted puede ayudar a reforzar lo estudiado pidiendo a su hijo o hija que le cuente lo que hacemos en la escuela y que le explique algunos de los dibujos y mapas en el libro.

Usted puede ayudar a su hijo o hija en casa con la siguiente actividad:

Por lo menos una vez a la semana, vean juntos las noticias y hagan una lista de varios lugares mencionados en el programa. Luego usen un atlas o un globo terráqueo para localizar por lo menos tres de los lugares. Finalmente, usen estos lugares para practicar alguna de las destrezas que se estén estudiando, como por ejemplo, decir si cada pais está en el Hemisferio Norte, Sur, Este u Oeste. En otra oportunidad, pida a su hijo o hija que determine la latitud y longitud de los mismos o de otros lugares. Más adelante, determine el huso horario y el clima de los lugares. Puede ayudar a su hijo o hija a investigar temas especiales y desarrollar mapas, cuadros o tablas acerca del lugar.

Gracias por su interés y apoyo.

Sinceramente,

Name _____

MAP ATTACK!

✔ <u>Read the title.</u>

1. What is the title? _____

2. What is one thing you might learn from this map?

_____

✔ <u>Read the map key.</u>

3. Draw two symbols from the map in the boxes. Write their names on the lines below.

_____   _____

✔ <u>Read the compass rose.</u>

4. Name something on the map in each direction.

North _____   South _____

East _____   West _____

✔ <u>Read the map scale.</u>

5. Use the map scale to measure the distance between two places on the map.

The distance from _____ to _____ is _____ miles.

✔ <u>Read the grid.</u>

6. How many squares are in each row? _____

7. How many squares are in each column? _____

8. Name one thing in A-1. _____

✔ <u>Draw a conclusion.</u>

9. Name one thing you learned from this map. _____

_____

Geography Themes Up Close

OBJECTIVES

Students will
◆ identify the physical features used by geographers to classify regions
◆ identify the human features used by geographers to classify regions
◆ draw inferences from maps of regions
◆ analyze maps to determine human and physical features of regions

MATERIALS NEEDED

several maps that show regions based on physical and human features
Blackline Master T35

INTRODUCING THE SKILL

◆ Ask students to identify political regions of which their community is part. Students may mention school district, township, county or parish, state, and country. Ask students to explain why their community is part of so many political regions. Explain that in this feature they will learn about some additional categories, besides political regions, that geographers use to determine regions.

TEACHING NOTES

Page 76   Read and discuss with students the introductory paragraph on page 76. Then ask students to name other physical features that could be used as the basis for naming regions. Next, ask students to name some other human features that could be used as bases for organizing regions.
◆ Bring to class several maps that show regions based on physical and human features. Allow students time to identify the criteria used to identify the regions. Point out that the criteria that can be used to identify regions is unlimited. Also remind students that the size of regions vary from small, such as neighborhoods, to large, such as continents.
◆ Have students look at the map of India on page 64. Ask students to name the characteristic that has been used to divide India into regions on this map. (*how the land is used*) Ask: In which region are the cities on the map? (*Farming land*) Have students compare this map with a landform map of India. Ask: In what kind of landform is the unproductive land located? (*Northwest is desert, other areas are part of The Himalaya*) In what kind of landform is the farming land? (*Plains, river valleys*)
◆ Have students look at the map on page 68. Ask: What characteristic has been used to organize these two maps of Italy into regions? (*Precipitation and resources*) When would it be important to know the precipitation regions of Italy? (*Answers will vary, but might include something like the following: A farmer needs to know the amount of precipitation in the area in order to know which crops would grow best.*)
Page 77   Have students share their answers to questions 5–9 on this page. Discuss the answers to the last question and accept any reasonable response. Point out to students that naming regions based on religion is just one of many human features used. Point out to students that the maps of Japan on page 68 and 69 shows regions based on human features. Ask: What are the human features used in these maps to organize regions? (*Population, land use, and products*)
◆ Ask students to look at the North American Time Zone map on page 72. Point out that this is a map of regions. Ask: Is this map based on physical or human features? (*Answers will vary, but students should point out that time is based on the rotation of Earth, which is a physical feature, but that humans have drawn the lines to make the time zones.*) Have them identify the time zone region of which they are part. Ask: Why is it important to divide the country into these regions?

EXTENSION ACTIVITIES

◆ Have students find other maps in *Maps•Globes•Graphs* that show regions. Ask them to analyze the maps to determine the physical and human features on which each map is based.
◆ Have students compare political maps of Eastern Europe and Russia today with political maps of the same area in the 1970s. Point out that regions change. Ask them to explain why these political regions changed. Then ask what factors can cause regions based on physical features to change. (*Students might indicate that regions based on physical features may change as a result of natural disasters such as forest fires, hurricanes, tornadoes, earthquakes, and volcanoes. They may also change as a result of human interaction with the environment, such as oil spills, acid rain, global warming, and changing the environment to meet needs and wants.*)

AT HOME ACTIVITY

◆ Provide students with copies of the blackline map of the world on page T35. Have students work with family members to research and show a region map. They may use either a physical feature or a human feature as the basis of their map.

OBJECTIVES

Students will
♦ identify a globe as the most accurate model of Earth
♦ recognize map projections as different ways that Earth can be shown on a flat surface
♦ recognize that every map projection is distorted in some way
♦ identify distortions on specific maps

MATERIALS NEEDED

balloons
Transparency 12
"New Perspective on the World," *National Geographic*, Dec. 1988, pp. 910–913

VOCABULARY

cartographers   Mercator projection
distortion   Robinson projection
projection   polar projection

INTRODUCING THE SKILL

♦ Provide students with balloons. Have students draw pictures and write words over most of the surface of the balloon. Then ask students to use paper to draw a picture that shows all sides of the balloon. Give students five or ten minutes to attempt this, then discuss the difficulties involved. Relate this exercise to a cartographer's difficulty in portraying Earth on a flat surface. Tell students that in Chapter 11 they will learn about some of the ways in which cartographers draw maps.
♦ Ask students to brainstorm a list of advantages maps have over globes. (*A map can be folded and easily taken from place to place, but a globe cannot. Maps are generally cheaper than globes. A map can show the whole Earth at one time. A globe shows only one side of Earth at a time. A globe must be turned to view the other side of Earth. A map can show a small part of Earth in large size, but a globe cannot.*) Ask students to name an advantage globes have over maps. (*Globes are models of Earth so they give a truer view of Earth than maps give.*)

TEACHING NOTES

Page 78   Use Transparency 12 with students as you introduce the information on this page.
Pages 78 and 79   After the students complete these two pages, have them locate Mercator, Robinson, and polar projections in their social studies text and in atlases. Ask them to determine the kinds of distortions that occur with the different types of projections.
Page 80   Tell students that a Mercator projection is a type of cylindrical projection. This means the projection is made as if a cylinder of paper were wrapped around the globe at the Equator. Demonstrate this by using a globe. Tell students that the meridians would be extended straight up and down in this projection and that land masses near the pole would appear much larger than they actually are. Have students compare the Mercator map on this page with a globe to see the lines of latitude and the distortions of the continents.
Page 81   Read the following article to students: "New Perspective on the World." *National Geographic*, Dec. 1998, pp. 910–913. The National Geographic Society's chief cartographer, John B. Garver, Jr., explains why the Society decided to use the Robinson projection for making a new world map.
Page 82   Point out to students that distances and directions are accurate on polar projections when the line of travel passes through the poles. Therefore, polar projections are often used in air navigation.

EXTENSION ACTIVITIES

♦ Have students research Gerhardus Mercator and his method of making maps.
♦ Divide the class into five groups. Assign each group one of the following map projections to research: Miller cylindrical projection, conic projection, sinusoidal projection, Goode's interrupted equal-area projection, and Gall-Peters projection. Students should make a picture showing their assigned projection and prepare a presentation that explains the usefulness of the projection and its inaccuracies or distortions.
♦ Have students work in groups of three to find the most direct route between any two points on the surface of Earth by using polar projections. Have students record the distance and direction of the route on the polar projection with the route on a globe. Discuss the distortions students find.
♦ Have students write to the National Aeronautics and Space Administration, 300 E Street SW, Washington, D.C., 20024-3210, for information regarding the purposes of the following satellites: Landsat 1 launched in 1972 and Landsat 2 launched in 1975.

AT HOME ACTIVITY

♦ Have students demonstrate map distortions to a family member by having the family member draw pictures over most of the surface of an orange. Then have the family member peel the orange, being careful to keep the peel all in one piece. Have students work with the family member to flatten the peel and discuss how and why the pictures change.

OBJECTIVES

Students will
◆ use graph attack skills to read bar graphs, circle graphs, line graphs, and tables
◆ draw conclusions after reading bar graphs, circle graphs, line graphs, and tables
◆ use map and graph skills to compare tables and maps

MATERIALS NEEDED

photos of each student
apples

VOCABULARY

bar graph   line graph
circle graph   table

INTRODUCING THE SKILL

◆ Have students make tangible graphs to introduce the graph chapter. For example, have each student bring in a picture of herself or himself. Then line the pictures up in columns based on hair color, eye color, or clothing color. You will have a class pictograph. Have students think of other tangible graphs they could make.

TEACHING NOTES

Page 84   Help students estimate the population of each continent. Then have students use the **Graph Attack!** skills on this page to read bar graphs in their basal text.
Page 85   Teach students the steps of graph making: **Step 1.** Ask a question. **Step 2.** Collect and organize the information. **Step 3.** Record and label the graph. Brainstorm a list of topics students would enjoy graphing. Then have students work with a partner to create their own graph.
Page 86   Help students understand that a circle graph shows how a whole amount is divided into parts. Divide and cut a large circle into the same number of pieces as the number of students in the class. Ask students to color their piece of the circle based on their favorite ice cream flavor: chocolate-brown, strawberry-red, vanilla-white. Collect the colored pieces and arrange the circle to show how the favorite ice cream flavors compare. Then help students figure the approximate percentage for each ice cream flavor. Example: If there are 30 students in the class and 10 chose chocolate as their favorite flavor, that is about 33 percent. (10 chocolate ÷ 30 students = .3333 or 33%)
Page 87   When using this page, you may need to direct students to the circle graph if they have difficulty with number 4d. Give students additional practice comparing a circle graph and a

bar graph. Have them compare the circle graph of world land area by continent on page 86 with the bar graph of world population by continent on page 84. Have students draw conclusions after comparing the graphs.
Page 88   Have students rank the cities from highest to lowest based on their populations in 1990 and 1995. Have them observe changes and discuss why they think they occurred. Have students predict the rank order of the cities in 2000 from highest to lowest based on the trends shown on the graph. Have volunteers read their predictions and explain their reasoning for their rankings.
Page 89   Have students explain the differences between bar, circle, and line graphs. Ask students, "Why are some graphs better than others for certain kinds of information?" Next, have students compare the climate graphs on this page with the climate map on page 53. Have students draw conclusions after comparing the graphs and the map.
Page 90   As students work number 4c on this page, you may need to point out how to compare the area and population of Brazil and Canada in order for them to determine which country has the greater population density. After students complete this page, have them use the **Table Attack!** skills on this page to read tables in their basal text.
Page 91   Give students additional practice comparing a table and a map by having students work with a partner to write questions such as those in number 4 on this page.

EXTENSION ACTIVITIES

◆ Combine this graph chapter with a science chapter. Have students graph the results of experiments.
◆ Give each student an apple to eat. Tell them to save and count the seeds. On the chalkboard, have students write their name and the number of seeds they found in their apple. Help students organize and graph this information.
◆ Divide the class into small groups. Have students use an encyclopedia, almanac or another source to find information about a state or a country. Ask them to organize this information in the form of a table and a map. Have students make up five questions that compare the table and the map. Have groups exchange tables, maps, and questions. Ask them to answer another group's questions.

AT HOME ACTIVITY

◆ Have students work with family members and friends to make a table showing information about these individuals, such as: name, date of birth, city of birth, favorite sports team, favorite book, favorite movie, favorite TV show, favorite song.

Date _____

Dear Family:

Throughout the school year, your child will be learning and practicing geography skills by using *Maps•Globes•Graphs, Level F.* In the twelve chapters, your child will learn to identify the continents, oceans, the North and South Poles, the Equator, and the hemispheres on a map and globe. Your child will also work with map keys, directions, scale and distance, and latitude and longitude to interpret various kinds of maps. Some of these include relief and elevation maps, climate maps, and special purpose maps that combine several different kinds of information. Your child also will study time zones and polar projections and will learn to understand and create various kinds of graphs and tables.

You can help your child reinforce what we study by asking him or her to talk to you about what we are doing. You might ask your child to explain to you some of the pictures and maps in the book.

You can help your child by engaging in the following activity at home to support and reinforce our study of these skills.

At least once each week watch an evening news program together and make a list of several places around the world that are mentioned. After the program, use an atlas or globe to locate at least three of those places. Then, use these places to practice the skill currently being studied. For example, have your child name whether each place is in the Northern or Southern Hemisphere, then in the Eastern or Western Hemisphere. Another time have your child determine the latitude and longitude of the same or different places. Later, determine the time zone and climate of the places. You could even help your child research special topics and develop special maps, charts, or tables about the place.

Thank you for your interest and support.

Sincerely,

_____

Fecha _____

Estimada familia:

A lo largo de este año escolar, su hijo o hija aprenderá y practicará destrezas de geografía usando *Maps•Globes•Graphs, Level F*. En los doce capítulos, su hijo o hija aprenderá a identificar los continentes, océanos, polos Norte y Sur, el Ecuador y los hemisferios en un mapa y en el globo terráqueo. Su hijo o hija también trabajará con claves de mapas, direcciones, escala y distancia y latitud y longitud para interpretar diferentes tipos de mapas. Algunos de éstos incluyen mapas de relieve y elevación, mapas de clima y mapas que combinan diferentes tipos de información. Su hijo o hija también estudiará el huso horario y proyecciones polares y llegará a comprender y crear varios tipos de gráficas y tablas.

Usted puede ayudar a reforzar lo estudiado pidiendo a su hijo o hija que le cuente lo que hacemos en la escuela y que le explique algunos de los dibujos y mapas en el libro.

Usted puede ayudar a su hijo o hija en casa con la siguiente actividad:

Por lo menos una vez a la semana, vean juntos las noticias y hagan una lista de varios lugares mencionados en el programa. Luego usen un atlas o un globo terráqueo para localizar por lo menos tres de los lugares. Finalmente, usen estos lugares para practicar alguna de las destrezas que se estén estudiando, como por ejemplo, decir si cada pais está en el Hemisferio Norte, Sur, Este u Oeste. En otra oportunidad, pida a su hijo o hija que determine la latitud y longitud de los mismos o de otros lugares. Más adelante, determine el huso horario y el clima de los lugares. Puede ayudar a su hijo o hija a investigar temas especiales y desarrollar mapas, cuadros o tablas acerca del lugar.

Gracias por su interés y apoyo.

Sinceramente,

Name _____

MAP ATTACK!

✔ <u>Read the title.</u>

    1. What is the title? _____

    2. What is one thing you might learn from this map?

    _____

✔ <u>Read the map key.</u>

    3. Draw two symbols from the map in the boxes. Write their names on the lines below.

    ☐ _____   ☐ _____

✔ <u>Read the compass rose.</u>

    4. Name something on the map in each direction.

    North _____   South _____

    East _____   West _____

✔ <u>Read the map scale.</u>

    5. Use the map scale to measure the distance between two places on the map.

    The distance from _____ to _____ is _____ miles.

✔ <u>Read the grid.</u>

    6. How many squares are in each row? _____

    7. How many squares are in each column? _____

    8. Name one thing in A-1. _____

✔ <u>Draw a conclusion.</u>

    9. Name one thing you learned from this map. _____

    _____

Name _____

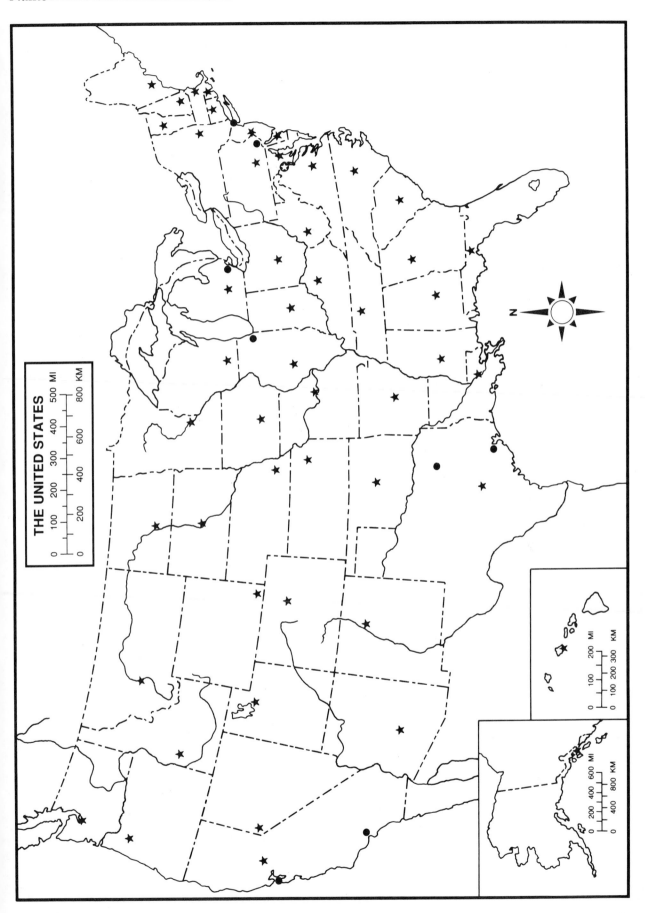

THE UNITED STATES

Name _____

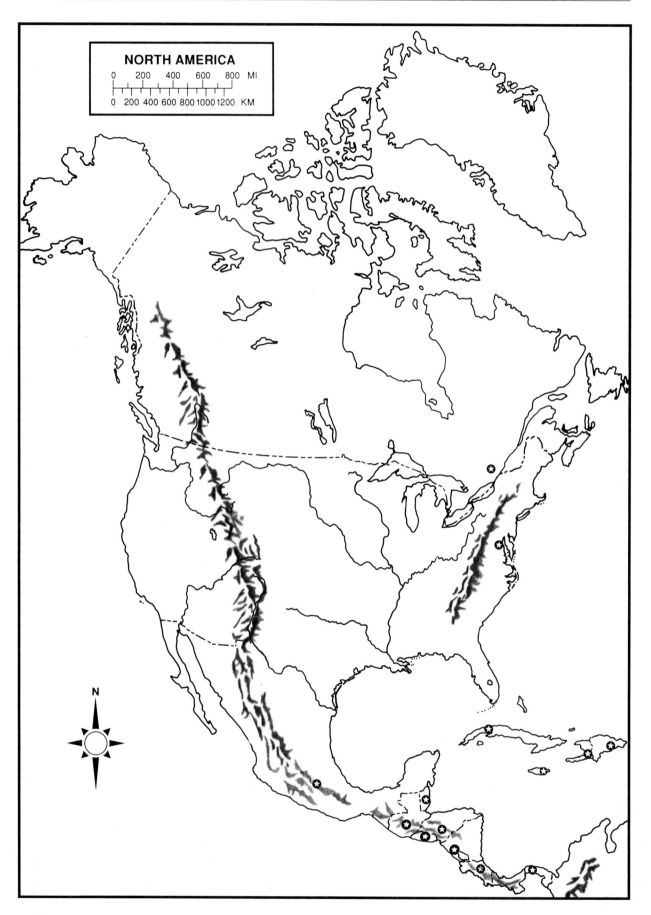

N

Name _____

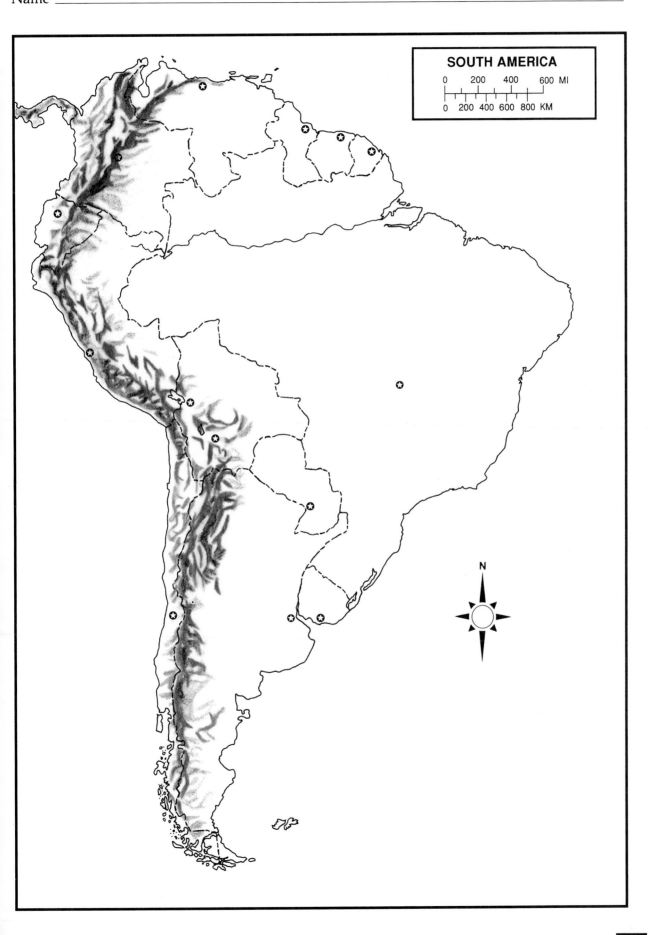

Name _____

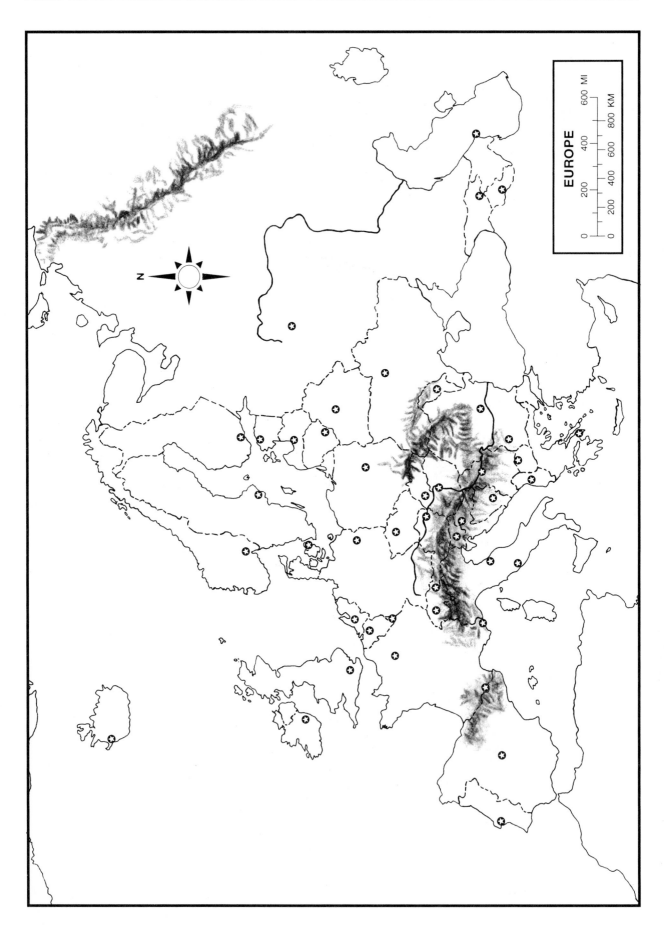

Name _____

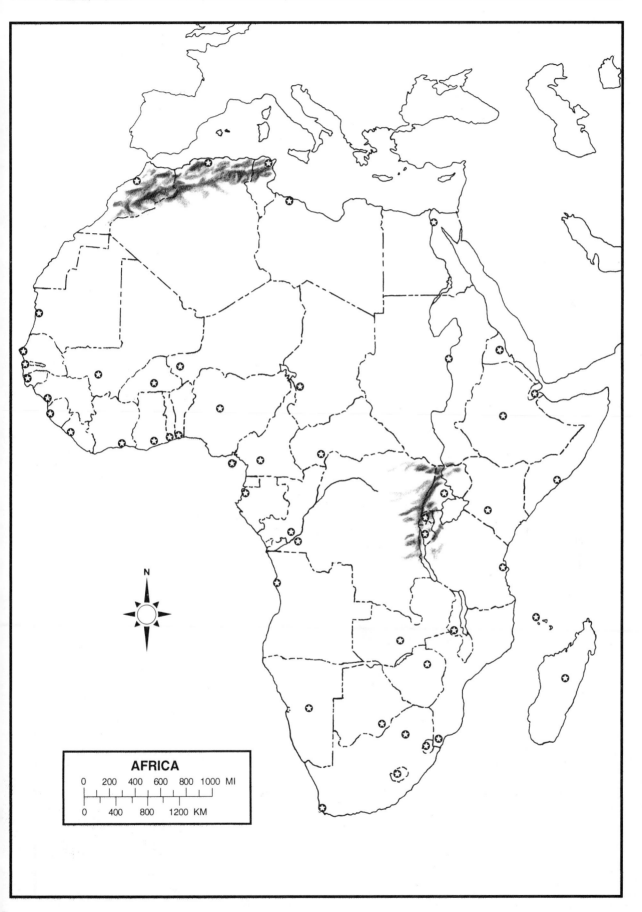

AFRICA

0   200   400   600   800   1000 MI

0   400   800   1200 KM

Name _____

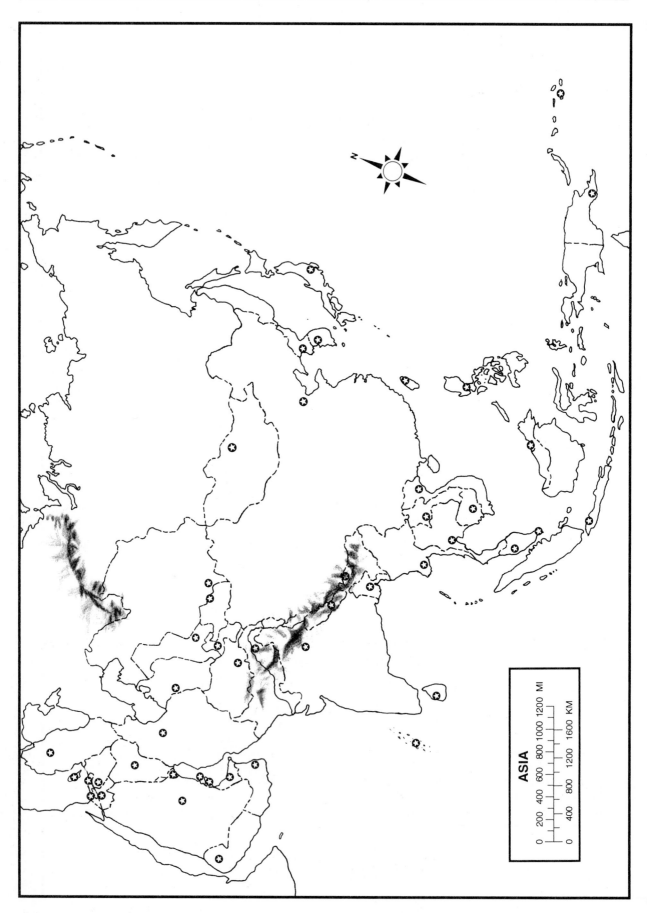

ASIA

0 200 400 600 800 1000 1200 MI

0   400   800   1200   1600 KM

Name _____

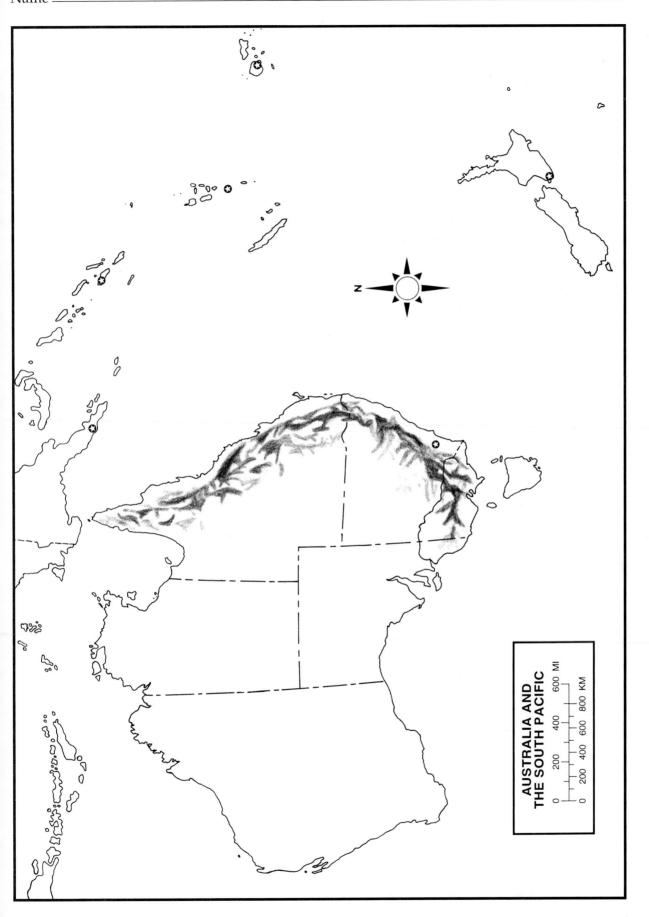

AUSTRALIA AND
THE SOUTH PACIFIC

600 MI
400
200
0

800 KM
600
400
200
0

Name _____

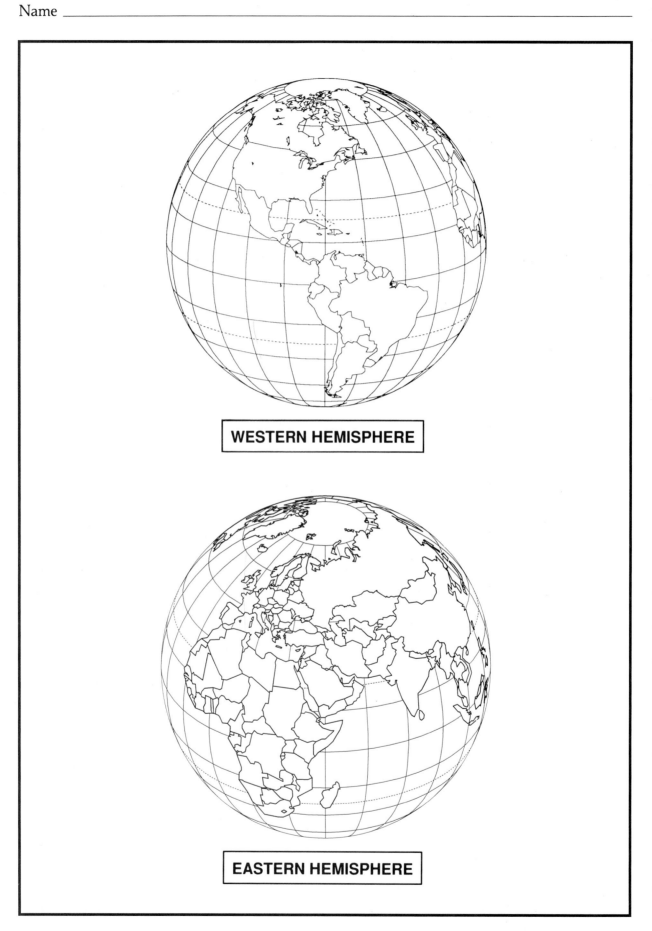

WESTERN HEMISPHERE

EASTERN HEMISPHERE

Name _____

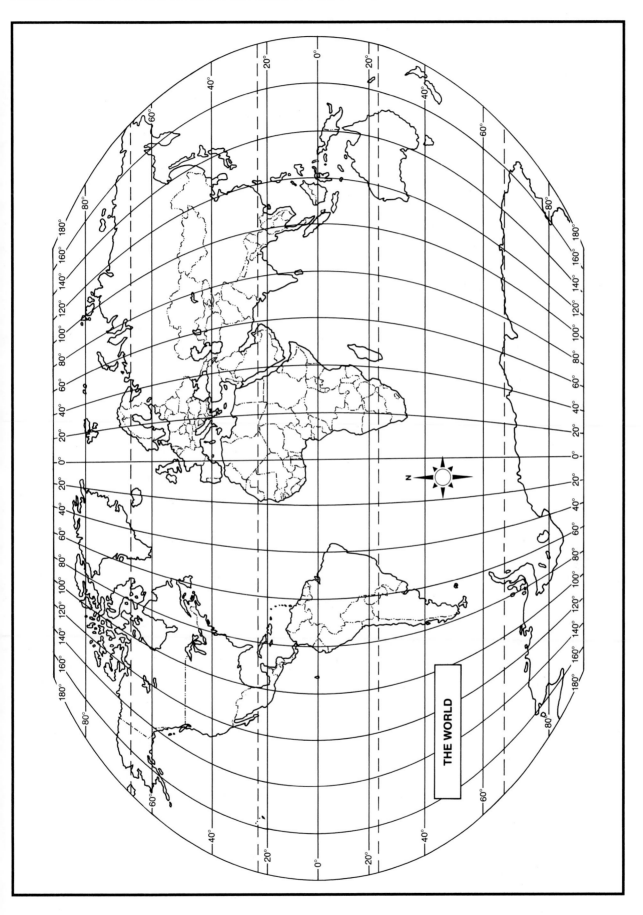

THE WORLD

Name _____

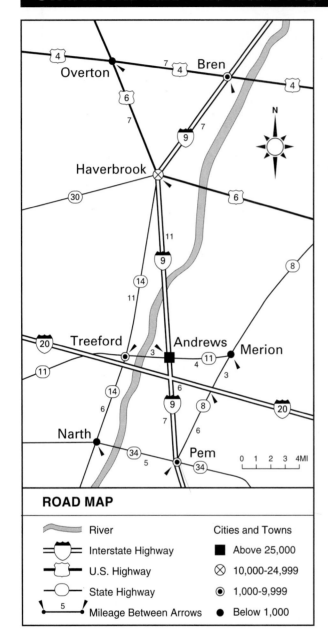

ROAD MAP

～～ River	Cities and Towns	
Interstate Highway	■	Above 25,000
U.S. Highway	⊗	10,000-24,999
State Highway	⊙	1,000-9,999
⌐5⌐ Mileage Between Arrows	●	Below 1,000

Use the two road maps on the left to answer the questions.

1. Where is the junction of U.S. Highway ⑧ and U.S. Highway ⑪?
Ⓐ West of Andrews
Ⓑ Merion
Ⓒ Pem
Ⓓ Treeford

2. What is the population of Narth?
Ⓐ Less than 1,000
Ⓑ 1,000–9,999
Ⓒ 10,000–24,999
Ⓓ More than 25,000

3. Which town probably has the most highway traffic?
Ⓐ Andrews
Ⓑ Bren
Ⓒ Haverbrook
Ⓓ Narth

4. If you left Pem and drove 25 miles north on Interstate 9, where would you be?
Ⓐ Andrews
Ⓑ Haverbrook
Ⓒ Overton
Ⓓ Bren

5. Where would this sign be found?

| Overton | 7 miles | → |
| Andrews | 11 miles | ← |

Ⓐ Treeford
Ⓑ Junction of ⑥ and ⑨
Ⓒ Bren
Ⓓ Junction of ⑪ and ⑭

6. In Treeford, the junction of state highways 11 and 14 is also the intersection of
Ⓐ Dogwood Ave. and Quail St.
Ⓑ Dogwood Ave. and Cedar Ave.
Ⓒ Quail St. and Birch Ave.
Ⓓ Birch Ave. and Robin St.

The maps below show four states of the imaginary country Bajon.

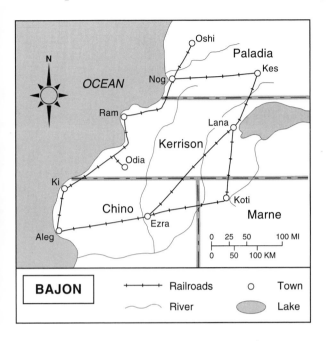

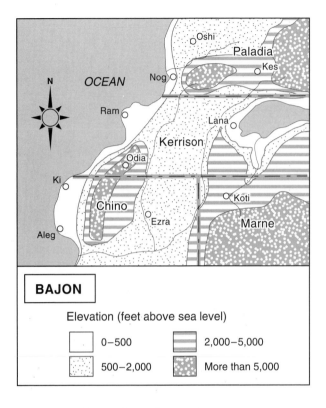

7. **Which state has the highest average elevation?**
   (A) Paladia
   (B) Kerrison
   (C) Chino
   (D) Marne

8. **Which statement best describes the elevation of the railroad line between Lana and Ezra?**
   (A) The elevation remains about the same.
   (B) The elevation sharply decreases.
   (C) The elevation steadily increases.
   (D) The elevation remains level and then sharply decreases.

9. **The rivers shown on the maps always flow**
   (A) From north to south
   (B) From south to north
   (C) From higher elevation to lower elevation
   (D) Through the same level of elevation

10. **The elevation of Kes is**
    (A) 0–500 feet
    (B) 500–2,000 feet
    (C) 2,000–5,000 feet
    (D) More than 5,000 feet

11. **Which section of the railroad was probably the most difficult to build?**
    (A) Lana to Kes
    (B) Koti to Lana
    (C) Ram to Nog
    (D) Ezra to Aleg

12. **About how far is it from Kes to Nog?**
    (A) 175 mi; 350 km
    (B) 125 mi; 190 km
    (C) 75 mi; 120 km
    (D) 50 mi; 80 km

Name

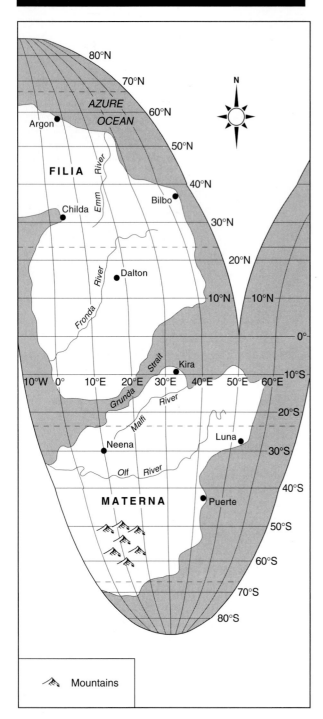

The map to the left shows an imaginary portion of the world.

1. **Which physical feature crosses the Tropic of Capricorn?**
   Ⓐ Emm River
   Ⓑ Grunda Strait
   Ⓒ Malfi River
   Ⓓ Materna Mountains

2. **Which of these cities is located near 40°N, 40°E?**
   Ⓐ Argon
   Ⓑ Bilbo
   Ⓒ Kira
   Ⓓ Luna

3. **When it is noon in Argon, in Neena it is probably**
   Ⓐ 6 A.M.
   Ⓑ 8 A.M.
   Ⓒ 12 P.M.
   Ⓓ 6 P.M.

4. **Which city probably has the coldest winter in December?**
   Ⓐ Argon
   Ⓑ Dalton
   Ⓒ Kira
   Ⓓ Luna

5. **Which of the following best describes the location of Neena?**
   Ⓐ 0°, 30°E
   Ⓑ 30°S, 50°E
   Ⓒ 30°N, 0°
   Ⓓ 30°S, 10°E

6. **In which city does the sun set first?**
   Ⓐ Bilbo
   Ⓑ Luna
   Ⓒ Neena
   Ⓓ Puerte

The maps below show four states of the imaginary country Bajon.

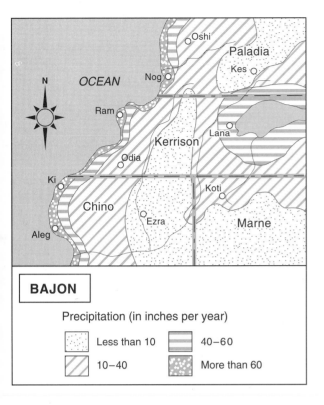

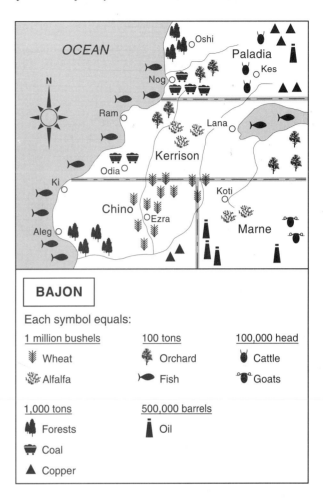

BAJON

Precipitation (in inches per year)

Less than 10   40–60

10–40   More than 60

BAJON

Each symbol equals:

1 million bushels	100 tons	100,000 head
Wheat	Orchard	Cattle
Alfalfa	Fish	Goats

1,000 tons	500,000 barrels
Forests	Oil
Coal	
Copper	

7. Which of the following cities receives the least amount of precipitation every year?
Ⓐ Oshi
Ⓑ Ram
Ⓒ Aleg
Ⓓ Ezra

8. What is the primary agricultural product grown in the state of Chino?
Ⓐ Alfalfa
Ⓑ Wheat
Ⓒ Orchards
Ⓓ Cattle

9. In which of the following cities is coal the most important resource?
Ⓐ Nog
Ⓑ Oshi
Ⓒ Koti
Ⓓ Kes

10. About how many tons of fish are caught each year from the ocean?
Ⓐ   200
Ⓑ   700
Ⓒ   900
Ⓓ 1,100

11. What is the annual precipitation in southern Marne?
Ⓐ Less than 10 inches
Ⓑ 10–40 inches
Ⓒ 40–60 inches
Ⓓ More than 60 inches

12. How much of Bajon's oil is produced in Paladia?
Ⓐ All
Ⓑ More than half
Ⓒ Half
Ⓓ Less than half

Standardized Tests/Answer Key

Level F of *Maps•Globes•Graphs* includes sample standardized tests on maps and globes. These tests will familiarize students with formats and directions for taking standardized tests. The Midterm Test, found on pages T36 and T37, reviews skills learned in Chapters 1 through 6. The Final Test, found on pages T38 and T39, focuses on skills learned in Chapters 7 through 11, but also encompasses skills learned and practiced in earlier chapters.

When you administer the tests, pass along the following tips to students.

1. Read the directions for each page carefully.
2. Remember your **Map Attack!** skills.
3. Decide which of the four answers is correct—A, B, C, or D.
4. Carefully fill in each answer circle completely. Press firmly with the pencil to make a dark mark.
5. If you finish the test before the time is up, go back and check your answers.

ANSWERS

Midterm Test

Page 36	1. B	2. A	3. C	4. D	5. B	6. A
Page 37	7. D	8. A	9. C	10. C	11. D	12. B

Final Test

Page 38	1. C	2. B	3. C	4. A	5. D	6. B
Page 39	7. D	8. B	9. A	10. C	11. A	12. D

Maps Globes Graphs

Level F

Writer
Henry Billings

Consultants

Marian Gregory
Teacher
San Luis Coastal Unified School District
San Luis Obispo, California

Gloria Sesso
Supervisor of Social Studies
Half Hollow Hills School District
Dix Hills, New York

Norman McRae, Ph.D.
Former Director of Fine Arts and Social Studies
Detroit Public Schools
Detroit, Michigan

Edna Whitfield
Former Social Studies Supervisor
St. Louis Public Schools
St. Louis, Missouri

Marilyn Nebenzahl
Social Studies Consultant
San Francisco, California

Karen Wiggins
Director of Social Studies
Richardson Independent School District
Richardson, Texas

Check the Maps•Globes•Graphs Website to find more fun geography activities at home.

Go to www.HarcourtAchieve.com/mggwelcome.html

Harcourt Achieve

Rigby • Steck-Vaughn

www.HarcourtAchieve.com
1.800.531.5015

Acknowledgments

Cartography   Land Registration and Information Service
                   Amherst, Nova Scotia, Canada
                   Gary J. Robinson
                   MapQuest.com, Inc.
                   R.R. Donnelley and Sons Company
                   XNR Productions Inc., Madison, Wisconsin

Photography Credits
COVER (globe, clouds): ©PhotoDisc; p. 4 ©Victor Brunelle Photography, Inc/Stock Boston; p. 5(t) ©Jeffrey Dunn/ Stock Boston; p. 5(b) ©PhotoDisc; p. 6 ©Jim Steinberg/Photo Researchers; p. 7(t) ©Kaz Chiba Photography/Liason International; p. 7(b) ©PhotoDisc.

Illustration Credits
Dennis Harms pp. 8, 9, 10, 11, 12, 13, 50, 71, 78; David Griffin p. 79 inset, p. 80 inset; Michael Krone p. 42

ISBN 0-7398-9106-5

© 2004 Harcourt Achieve Inc.

10 11 12 13 14 15   1678   17 16 15 14 13 12
4500345891

Contents

Geography Themes 4

   1 • Globes 8

   2 • Symbols and Directions 14

Geography Themes Up Close: Movement 20

   3 • Scale and Distance 22

   4 • Route Maps 28

Geography Themes Up Close: Place 34

   5 • Relief and Elevation 36

   6 • Latitude and Longitude 42

Geography Themes Up Close: Location 48

   7 • Climate Maps 50

   8 • Combining Maps 56

Geography Themes Up Close: Human/Environment Interaction 62

   9 • Comparing Maps 64

  10 • Time Zones 70

Geography Themes Up Close: Regions 76

  11 • Projections 78

  12 • Graphs 84

Atlas 92

Glossary 95

Geography Themes

In *Maps•Globes•Graphs* you will learn about some of the tools that scientists use to study **geography**. Geography is the study of Earth and the ways people use Earth to live and work. There are five themes, or topics, to help people organize ideas as they study geography.

The Five Themes of Geography
- **Location**
- **Place**
- **Human/Environment Interaction**
- **Movement**
- **Regions**

Location

Location describes where something can be found. One way to describe the location of something is to use an address. Another way is to name what something is near.

 Based on what you see in this photograph, describe the location of Jackson Middle School.

Jackson Middle School is on a street in an area near many trees and

houses.

Place

Place describes the **physical features** and **human features** of a location. The physical features of a location are natural features that include the climate, landforms, soil, bodies of water, and plants and animals. The human features are those made by people, such as population, jobs, language, customs, religion, and government.

 How would you describe Rio de Janeiro, Brazil?

Answers will vary, but students might say it is a large city, located on

hills near water; it has varied architecture and many buildings.

Human/Environment Interaction

Human/Environment Interaction describes how the environment affects people and how people affect the environment. This theme also describes how people depend upon the environment. For example, some people depend on lakes to provide them with drinking water.

Human/Environment Interaction describes how people adapt to their environment.

 The people in this photograph live in Egypt, which has a hot, dry climate. How do you think their clothing helps them adapt to their climate?

Answers will vary, but students should observe that clothes that are light-

colored and lightweight, as well as loose-fitting, help keep the wearer

more cool and comfortable in hot, dry climates.

Human/Environment Interaction also describes how people change the environment to meet their needs and wants. Some changes may be harmful to the environment. For example, clearing land of all trees may cause soil erosion. Other changes people make can be beneficial.

 How are irrigation systems helpful in areas of little rain?

Irrigation provides the water necessary to grow crops when there is little

rain.

Movement

Movement describes how and why people, goods, information, and ideas move from place to place. Movement is often described in terms of transportation and communication. Highways, railroads, and rivers are examples of transportation networks that move people and goods from place to place. Television, newspapers, and computers are examples of communication tools that move information and ideas from place to place.

 Explain the kind of movement represented in this photograph.

Answers will vary, but students should recognize that both the truck and

the barge are moving goods.

Regions

Regions describe places on Earth with similar features. Physical features, such as landforms, natural resources, or climate can describe a region. The Amazon River basin is a region defined by its physical feature—the Amazon River. Human features, such as politics, religion, customs, or language, can also describe a region. Canada is a region described by political divisions called provinces. Regions can be large, such as the Eastern Hemisphere, or small, such as a neighborhood.

 How would you describe the region shown in this photograph? List a physical or human feature that defines the region.

Answers will vary. Accept all reasonable answers. Students might answer that

the region is marked by physical features—steep canyons and rock formations.

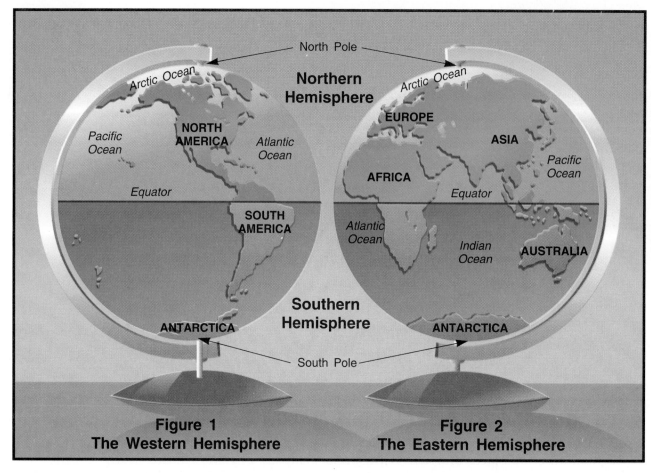

Figure 1
The Western Hemisphere

Figure 2
The Eastern Hemisphere

A **globe** is a model of Earth, which is shaped somewhat like a sphere, or ball. Globes show **continents** and **oceans**, the large land and water masses on Earth. Find the seven continents and four oceans on Figures 1 and 2 above.

Some points and imaginary lines help us find places on Earth. The **North Pole** and the **South Pole** are the places farthest north and south on Earth. We use the poles to know the four main directions, north, south, east, and west.

Find the **Equator** on Figures 1 and 2. This imaginary circle around the middle of Earth divides Earth into two hemispheres. **Hemisphere** means half a sphere or globe. The hemisphere north of the Equator is called the **Northern Hemisphere**. The hemisphere south of the Equator is called the **Southern Hemisphere**.

The globe can also be divided into the **Eastern Hemisphere** and the **Western Hemisphere**. Figure 1 shows the Western Hemisphere. Figure 2 shows the Eastern Hemisphere.

► If you stand on the North Pole, what is the only direction you can go? south
If you stand on the South Pole, what is the only direction you can go? north

► Name the seven continents and the four oceans. North and South America, Antarctica, Europe, Africa, Asia, Australia; Atlantic, Pacific, Arctic, Indian Ocean
Which continents and oceans are in the Eastern Hemisphere? Europe, Asia, Africa, Australia, Antarctica; Atlantic, Pacific, Arctic, and Indian Oceans
Which are in the Western Hemisphere? North America, South America, Antarctica; Atlantic, Pacific, and Arctic Oceans

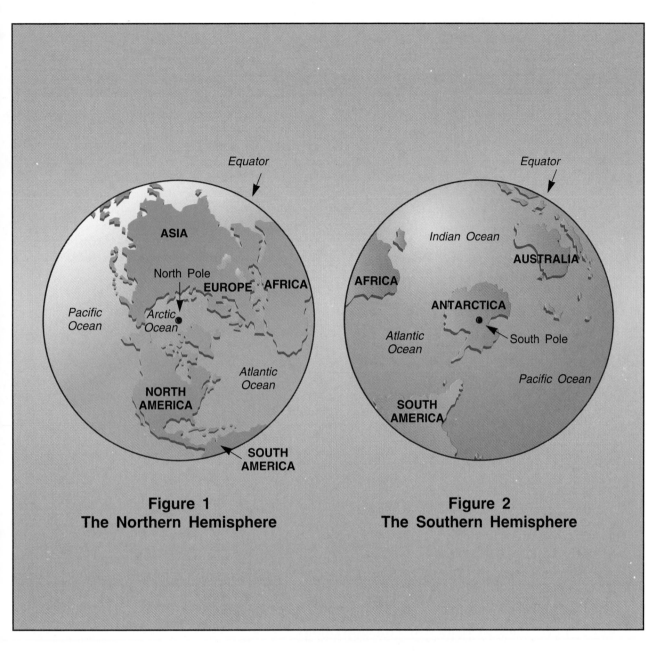

Figure 1
The Northern Hemisphere

Figure 2
The Southern Hemisphere

Figures 1 and 2 show a different way of looking at the Northern and Southern Hemispheres. Figure 1 shows the Northern Hemisphere with the North Pole in the center. What continents do you recognize? Look back at the hemispheres on page 8 to help you identify the continents.

Figure 2 shows the Southern Hemisphere with the South Pole in the center. The South Pole is on which continent? What other continents do you see? **Antarctica; Africa, Australia, South America**

► Can you find the Equator on both Figure 1 and Figure 2?

► Which oceans are in the Southern Hemisphere? Which are in the Northern? **Southern: Atlantic, Pacific, Indian Northern: Atlantic, Pacific, Arctic, Indian**
Which continents are entirely in the Southern Hemisphere? **Australia, Antarctica**
Which continents are entirely in the Northern Hemisphere? **Europe, North America, Asia**
Which have parts in both the Northern and Southern Hemispheres? **South America, Africa**

► Most of the land is in which hemisphere? **Northern**
Most of the water is in which hemisphere? **Southern**

Mastering the Eastern and Western Hemispheres

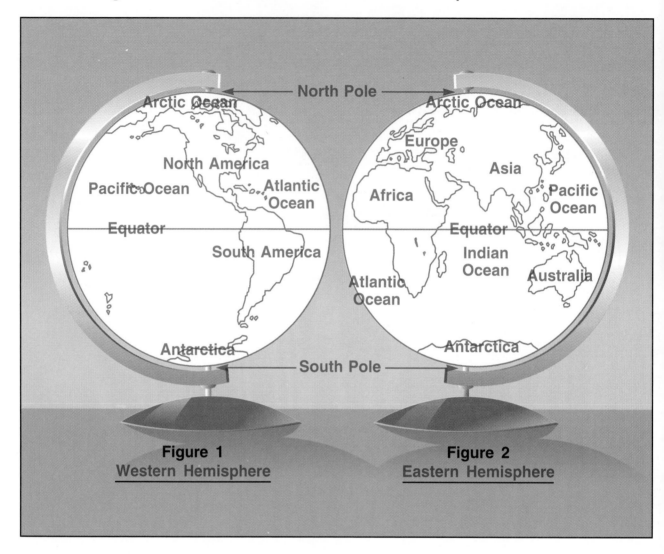

Figure 1
Western Hemisphere

Figure 2
Eastern Hemisphere

1. Label the Eastern and Western Hemispheres on the lines under Figures 1 and 2. Look back at page 8 if you need help.
2. Label the North Pole, South Pole, and Equator on each globe.
3. Label the continents and oceans on Figures 1 and 2. Again, look back at page 8 if you need help.
4. Which two continents are entirely in the Western Hemisphere?

   _____North America and South America_____

5. Which four continents are entirely or mostly in the Eastern

   Hemisphere? _____Europe, Asia, Africa, and Australia_____

   _____

6. Which continent is almost evenly divided between the Eastern and

   Western Hemispheres? _____Antarctica_____

7. Which ocean is entirely in the Eastern Hemisphere? ____Indian Ocean____

Mastering the Northern and Southern Hemispheres

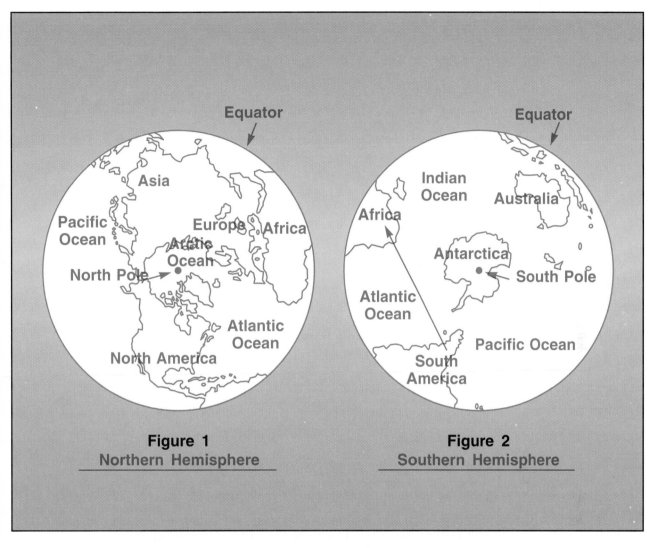

Figure 1
Northern Hemisphere

Figure 2
Southern Hemisphere

1. Label the North Pole, the South Pole, and the Equator on each globe. Look back at page 9 if you need help.
2. Label the Northern and Southern Hemispheres on the lines under Figures 1 and 2.
3. Label the continents and oceans on each hemisphere.
4. From the South Pole, the only direction you can go is _____**north**_____.
5. From the North Pole, the only direction you can go is _____**south**_____.
6. Which two continents are only in the Southern Hemisphere?
   Antarctica, Australia
7. Which three continents are only in the Northern Hemisphere?
   Europe, Asia, and North America
8. Draw an arrow pointing from South America to Africa on Figure 2.

   Which direction is that arrow pointing? _____**east**_____

Mastering the Four Hemispheres

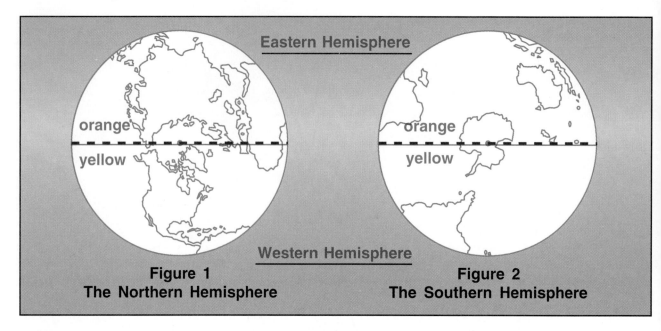

Eastern Hemisphere

orange

yellow

orange

yellow

Western Hemisphere

Figure 1
The Northern Hemisphere

Figure 2
The Southern Hemisphere

1. Figures 1 and 2 show the Northern and Southern Hemispheres. But the Eastern and Western Hemispheres are also part of these globes. Connect the dotted line on each globe to show the Eastern and Western Hemispheres. Color the western halves yellow. Color the eastern halves orange.

2. Label the Western Hemisphere and Eastern Hemisphere on the lines where they belong.

3. What point is at the center of the Northern Hemisphere? ___North Pole___

4. What point is at the center of the Southern Hemisphere? ___South Pole___

5. Find each place listed below in at least two of the hemispheres shown above. Some continents and oceans are in three or four hemispheres. Name the hemispheres in which you find each place.

   a. North America: ___Northern and Western Hemispheres___

   b. Pacific Ocean: ___Northern, Southern, Western, and Eastern Hemispheres___

   c. Arctic Ocean: ___Northern, Eastern, and Western Hemispheres___

   d. Europe: ___Northern, Eastern, and Western Hemispheres___

   e. Atlantic Ocean: ___Northern, Southern, Eastern, and Western Hemispheres___

   f. Australia: ___Southern and Eastern Hemispheres___

   g. Indian Ocean: ___Southern, Eastern, and Northern Hemispheres___

   h. Africa: ___Southern, Northern, Eastern, and Western Hemispheres___

   i. Asia: ___Northern, Eastern, and Western Hemispheres___

Skill Check

Vocabulary Check

North Pole	South Pole	globe
Equator	hemispheres	oceans
continents		

Write the word or phrase that makes each sentence true.

1. The _____ **North Pole** _____ is the place farthest north on Earth.

2. The Equator divides Earth into two _____ **hemispheres** _____.

3. A _____ **globe** _____ is a model that shows the shape of Earth.

4. Earth's _____ **continents** _____ and _____ **oceans** _____ are large land and water masses.

Globe Check

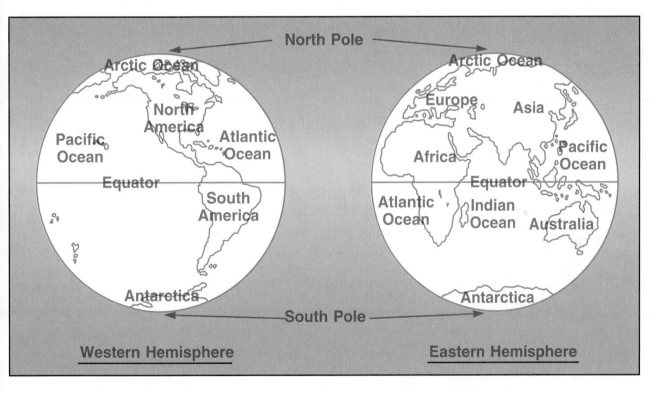

1. Label the hemispheres you see. Then label the continents, the oceans, the poles, and the Equator on each globe.

2. Which three continents are closest to the North Pole? _____
   North America, Europe, and Asia

3. Besides Antarctica, which three continents are closest to the South Pole?
   South America, Africa, and Australia

4. What point on Earth is farthest from the North Pole?
   the South Pole

THE UNITED STATES

— - - — International boundary

— - — State boundary

◉ National capital

★ State capital

A **map** is a flat drawing of any place. To understand a map, you must read it. Follow these steps to read and understand a map.

MAP ATTACK!

- **Read the title.** Just as a book's title tells you what you are reading, a map's title tells you what the map shows. What does this map's title tell you?
- **Read the map legend.** The legend, or key, explains the symbols on the map. What symbols are in the map legend? Find examples of each symbol on the map.
- **Read the compass rose.** The compass rose always shows north. The north arrow points to the North Pole. Once you find north you can find the other **cardinal directions**, east (E), west (W), and south (S). The compass rose often shows the **intermediate directions**: northwest (NW), southwest (SW), northeast (NE), and southeast (SE). Find the compass rose on the map. Then find each direction.

► From the capital city of Kentucky, in what direction is the capital of each of these states: Indiana, South Carolina, Ohio, Virginia, Tennessee, and Florida? Frankfort, Kentucky to: Indianapolis, Indiana—northwest; Columbia, South Carolina— southeast; Columbus, Ohio—northeast; Richmond, Virginia—east; Nashville, Tennessee— southwest; Tallahassee, Florida—southeast

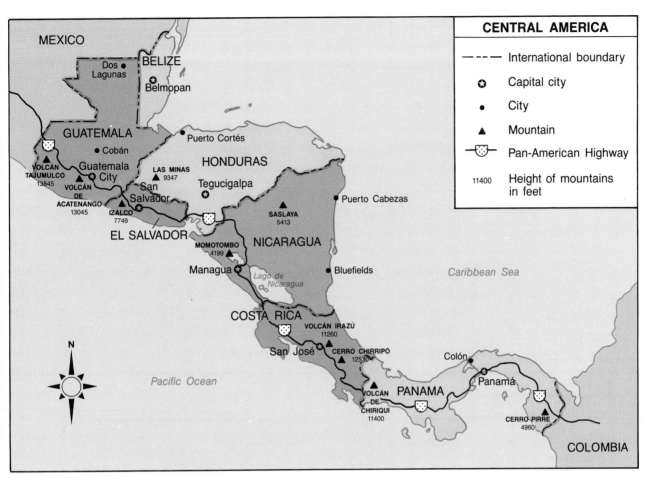

Not all maps show the same information. The title tells you the kind of information you can learn from the map. The legend explains the special symbols used on the map. Follow the **Map Attack!** steps to understand the information on this map.

MAP ATTACK!

- **Read the title.** What part of the world is shown on this map?
- **Read the legend.** What major highway is shown on this map? What kind of landform is shown?
- **Read the compass rose.** Where is the North Pole from Central America?

Notice on the map above that the labels are not all the same size. Labels for the largest places on a map are usually large and sometimes are shown in all capital letters. Labels for water are often blue.

▶ What countries make up Central America? El Salvador, Nicaragua, Costa Rica, Belize, Guatemala, Honduras, Panama

▶ The Pan American Highway crosses which countries? Mexico, Guatemala, El Salvador, Honduras, Nicaragua, Costa Rica, Panama, Colombia

▶ Which country has the highest mountains? Guatemala
How high are they? How do you know? 13,845 and 13,045 feet; The height of each mountain is labeled.

▶ Which mountain is farthest east? Cerro Pirre

Mastering Symbols and Directions

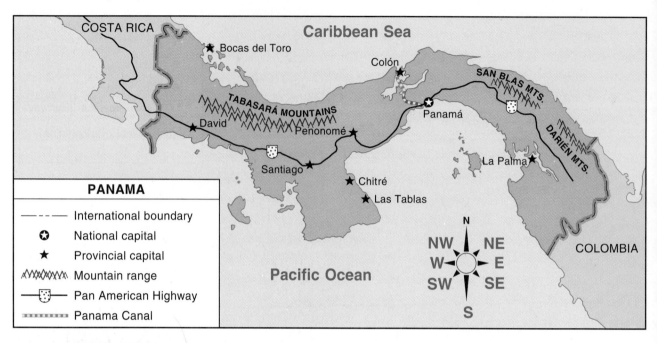

MAP ATTACK!

- **Read the title.** This map shows _____ Panama _____.
- **Read the legend.** What symbols are in the legend? Find an example of each symbol on the map.
- **Read the compass rose.** Find north. Then label the remaining points.

1. Label these bodies of water. Look back at page 15 for help.

    Caribbean Sea   Pacific Ocean

2. What country borders Panama on the east? _____ Colombia _____

3. What country borders Panama on the west? _____ Costa Rica _____

4. How many mountain ranges are shown on the map? _____ three _____

5. Find these pairs of places on the map. What direction would you travel to get from the first place to the second place? Write the abbreviation of the correct cardinal or intermediate direction.

    a. Bocas del Toro to David   S

    b. Santiago to Penonomé   NE

    c. the national capital to La Palma   SE

    d. Colón to Chitré   SW

    e. Las Tablas to Santiago   NW

6. Is the Pan American Highway north or south of the mountain ranges? ___ S ___

Mastering Symbols and Directions

THE CANADA/ UNITED STATES BORDER

- – – – International boundary
- –·–·– Provincial or state boundary
- ◉ National capital
- ★ Provincial or state capital

MAP ATTACK!

Follow the steps on page 16 to begin reading this map.

1. Trace the boundary between Canada and the United States in red.
2. Trace the state and province boundaries in green.   **colored and labeled to**
3. Label these capital cities.   **match directions**

   Salem, Oregon   Regina, Saskatchewan
   Quebec, Quebec   Helena, Montana

4. Victoria, British Columbia, is on Vancouver Island. Label Vancouver Island.
5. What state and province does the Columbia River flow through?

   Washington and British Columbia
   _____

6. What large lake is in central Manitoba? _____ **Lake Winnipeg** _____
7. Lake Superior forms a boundary for what states and province?

   Minnesota, Wisconsin, Michigan, and Ontario
   _____

8. What island is in James Bay? _____ **Akimiski Island** _____

9. What direction would you travel to get from Lansing to Toronto? __ **NE** __

   From Manitoba to Alberta? __ **W** __

10. The Red River forms a boundary between what two states?

    Minnesota and North Dakota
    _____

Mastering Directions on a Map

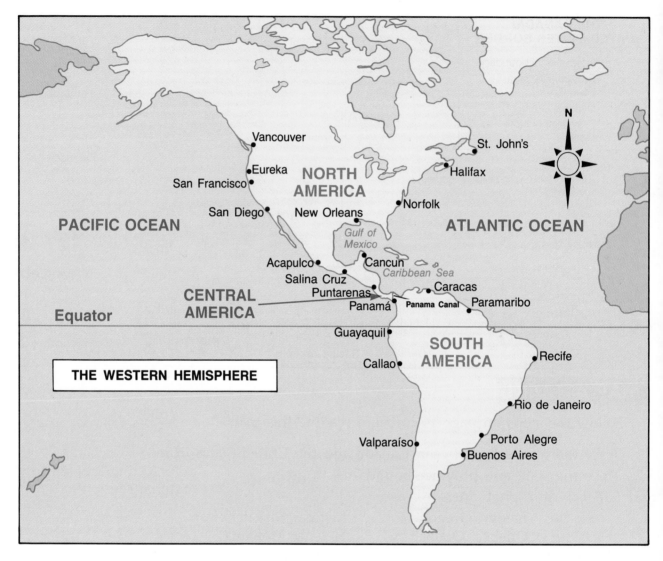

1. Write the following labels where they belong on this map.
   NORTH AMERICA   SOUTH AMERICA   CENTRAL AMERICA
   ATLANTIC OCEAN   Equator   PACIFIC OCEAN

2. Plan an ocean cruise along the western coast of North America.
   Begin in Vancouver. Name, in order, four other port cities on your
   route. **Answers should include four of the following: Eureka, San
   Francisco, San Diego, Acapulco, Salina Cruz**

3. Sail from the western coast to the eastern coast through the

   Panama Canal. What body of water do you enter? _____**Caribbean Sea**_____

4. Continue sailing south along the eastern coast of South America.
   Name, in order, four port cities along this route.
   **Answers should include four of the following: Caracas, Paramaribo, Recife, Rio de
   Janeiro, Porto Alegre, Buenos Aires**

5. Trace your route from Vancouver to Buenos Aires in red. Circle the
   cities on the route. **drawn to match directions**

Skill Check

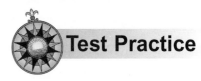

Vocabulary Check   **map**   **title**   **compass rose**

                                  intermediate directions   **legend**   **cardinal directions**

Write the word or phrase that best completes each sentence.

1. A _____ map _____ is a flat drawing of a place.

2. North, south, east, and west are _____ cardinal directions _____.

3. You can find north on a map by looking at the _____ compass rose _____.

4. The map's _____ legend _____ explains the map's symbols.

5. The map's _____ title _____ tells you what the map shows.

Map Check

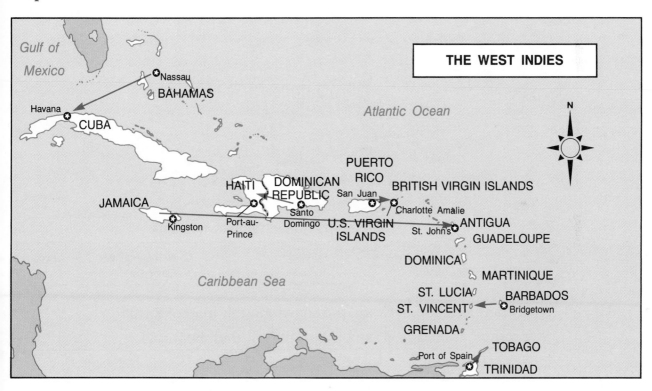

1. Highlight each of these countries using a separate, light color.

      Cuba   Jamaica   Haiti   Dominican Republic **colored to match directions**

2. On the map, draw an arrow from the first place to the second place in each pair. In which direction does each arrow point? Write the correct abbreviation for each direction below.

Nassau to Havana _**SW**_   Dominican Republic to Haiti _**W**_

Bridgetown to St. Vincent _**W**_   Jamaica to Antigua _**E**_

San Juan to Charlotte Amalie _**E**_   Trinidad to Tobago _**NE**_

Geography Themes Up Close

Movement describes the ways that people, goods, information, and ideas move from place to place. How do you get to and from school? Where do goods that you buy come from? How do you know what is going on in your community and in other parts of the world? These kinds of questions are answered in the study of movement. Movement happens through transportation and communication.

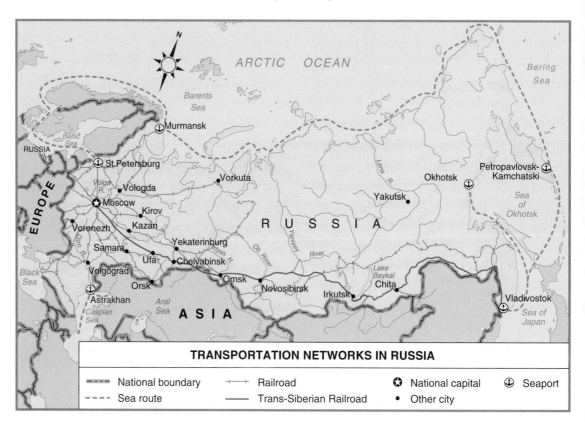

TRANSPORTATION NETWORKS IN RUSSIA

----- National boundary	⊢──┼─ Railroad	✪ National capital ⚓ Seaport
---- Sea route	── Trans-Siberian Railroad	• Other city

1. What transportation networks are shown on this map of Russia?

   Sea routes, railroads, Trans-Siberian Railroad, seaports,

   inland waterways

2. According to the map, how do people in Murmansk get goods to Vladivostock?

   Sea routes or the Trans-Siberian Railroad and other railroads

3. What means of transportation connects Russia's east coast with its western border?

   The Trans-Siberian Railroad

4. Based on the map, in what part of Russia would it be most difficult to transport people and goods? Why?

The northeastern part of Russia has no railroads and only

the Lena River that could be used for transportation.

Charts show facts organized and arranged in columns and rows. The chart below shows the number of some communication tools in various countries.

Communication Tools In Selected Countries

Country	Number of televisions per 1,000 people	Number of radios per 1,000 people	Number of newspapers per 1,000 people
Brazil	223	434	40
China	321	335	25
France	595	946	218
Algeria	223	242	38
Russia	410	417	105
United States	806	2,116	212

5. Which two countries have the fewest communication tools per 1,000 people?

China and Algeria

6. How might the information in the chart help geographers study the movement of information and ideas ?

The information shows how many people in each country have access

to communication. It is likely that the fewer people that have access to

communication tools, the less the movement of ideas and information.

 # Scale and Distance

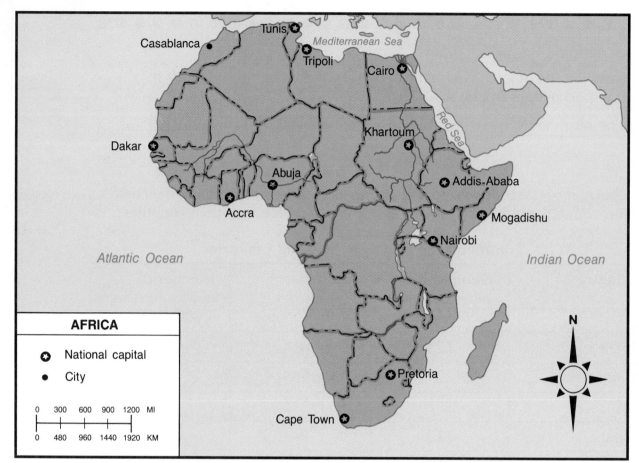

Maps can show the actual shape of a place. They cannot show the actual size of a place. The size of the place must be reduced to fit on a piece of paper. To help us figure distances, maps are drawn to scale. Scale is used to keep the shape of a place <u>and</u> show the distances. On the map of Africa above, the scale is "1 inch = 1,200 miles or 1,920 kilometers." A **map scale** shows the relationship of the actual distance on Earth to the distance on a map.

Map scales often show distance in miles (MI) and kilometers (KM). Find the map scale on the map above.

Miles and **kilometers** are two units of length used to measure distance. In the United States, distances are usually measured in miles. In many other countries the usual measurement is kilometers.

Find Dakar and Accra on the map of Africa above. They are only one inch apart. But how far apart are they on Earth? To find out, use the map scale and a ruler, a string, or the edge of a paper to figure the number of miles or kilometers between Dakar and Accra. The distance is about 1,200 miles or 1,920 kilometers.

► What is the distance between Khartoum and Addis Ababa?
Find the distance in miles and kilometers. **about 600 miles; about 960 kilometers**

► What is the distance between Tripoli and Cape Town?
Find the distance in miles and in kilometers. **about 4,500 miles; about 7,200 kilometer**

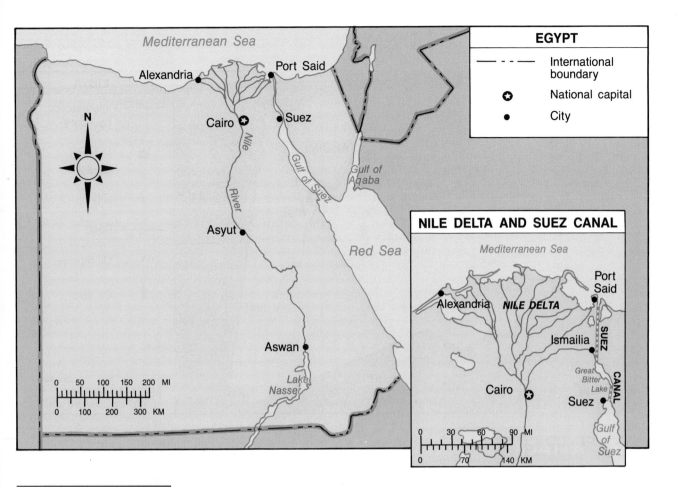

EGYPT

— - - —	International boundary
⊙	National capital
●	City

NILE DELTA AND SUEZ CANAL

MAP ATTACK! Add a step to read the maps.

- **Read the title.** What can you learn from these maps?
- **Read the legend.** Find each symbol on the maps.
- **Read the compass rose.** Find north on each map.
- **Read the map scales.** How does the scale differ on each map?

The scale is not the same on all maps. Look at the two maps above. The larger map shows all of Egypt. The smaller map is an inset map that shows only part of Egypt: the Nile Delta and the Suez Canal. An **inset map** is a small map within a larger map. An inset map may have its own scale.

► Compare the scales on the two maps.

► Measure the distance between Suez and Port Said on the map of Egypt. What is the distance? **about 100 miles**

► Measure the distance between Suez and Port Said on the inset map. What is the distance? **about 100 miles**

► On which map is it easier to measure distances? **the inset map**

► Can you measure the distance between Ismailia and Asyut? Why or why not? **No, both places are not shown on a single map.**

► How could you figure the distance between Ismailia and Asyut using both of the maps? **Use the inset map to measure the distance between Ismailia and Suez. Use the map of Egypt to measure the distance between Suez and Asyut.**

Scale and Distance **23**

Finding Distances in Libya

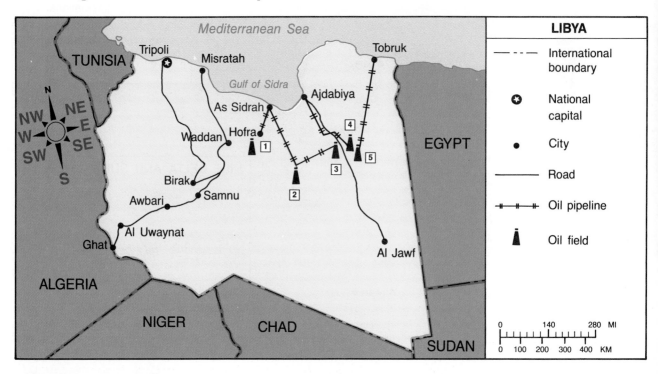

MAP ATTACK!

- **Read the title.** This map shows _____Libya_____.
- **Read the legend.** Check (✔) each symbol in the legend and a matching symbol on the map.
- **Read the compass rose.** Complete the compass rose.
- **Read the map scale.** The length of the scale stands for how many miles _about 280_? how many kilometers? _about 450_

1. Trace each oil pipeline. Then find its length.

    a. Hofra to As Sidrah   __about 150__ KM   __about 70__ MI   **All answers here are approximate.**

    b. Oil field #2 to As Sidrah   __about 300__ KM   __about 190__ MI

    c. Oil field #4 to Ajdabiya   __about 300__ KM   __about 190__ MI

    d. Oil field #5 to Tobruk   __about 450__ KM   __about 280__ MI

2. a. Which oil pipeline covers the longest distance?

    _____**Oil field #5 to Tobruk**_____

    b. Which oil pipeline covers the shortest distance?

    _____**Hofra to As Sidrah**_____

3. Draw a conclusion. Where do all the oil pipelines in Libya go?

    _____**to the coast**_____ Why? Answers may include the following: Oil can be transported on tankers; Cities on the coast may have industries or refineries.

Finding Distances in Southern Africa

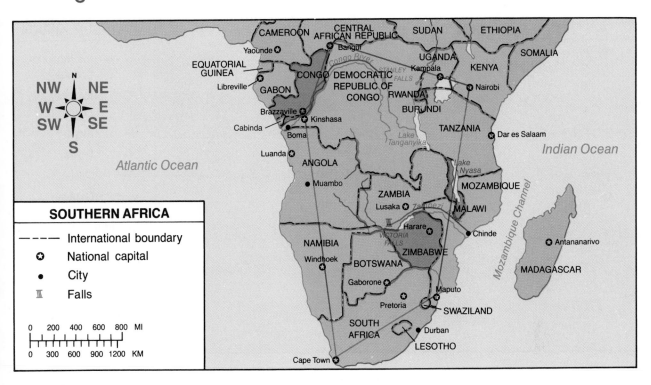

MAP ATTACK!

Follow the steps on page 24 to begin reading this map.

1. Draw a line from the first place to the second. Then find the distance.

   a. Cape Town to Windhoek __about 1,300__ KM __about 800__ MI   **All answers here**
   are approximate.

   b. Windhoek to Kinshasa __about 2,000__ KM __about 1,250__ MI

   c. Kinshasa to Bangui __about 1,000__ KM __about 650__ MI

   d. Bangui to Kampala __about 1,600__ KM __about 1,000__ MI

   e. Kampala to Nairobi __about 400__ KM __about 300__ MI

   f. Nairobi to Maputo __about 2,800__ KM __about 1,700__ MI

   g. Maputo to Cape Town __about 1,600__ KM __about 1,000__ MI

2. What is the total distance of this trip? __about 10,700__ KM __about 6,700__ MI

3. Trace the Congo River from Stanley Falls to Boma.

   Use the map scale to estimate this distance. __about 1,700__ KM __about 1,100__ MI

4. Trace the Zambezi River from Victoria Falls to Chinde.

   Use the map scale to estimate this distance. __about 1,400__ KM __about 900__ MI

5. Which river trip is longer? _____ **The Congo River trip is longer.**

Finding Distances in Northern Africa

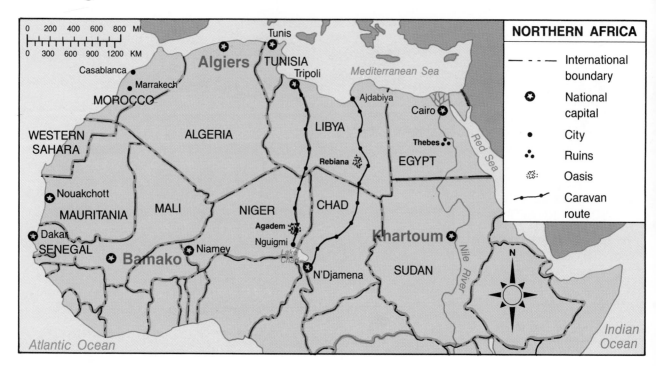

1. The Mediterranean Sea is a boundary for what countries? _____

   Egypt, Algeria, Tunisia, Libya, Morocco

2. Label these capital cities.
   a. Algiers, Algeria
   b. Khartoum, Sudan
   c. Bamako, Mali

3. Trace the caravan route from Tripoli, Libya to Nguigmi, Niger.

   a. What direction does it go? _____ **south** _____

   b. What oasis does it pass by? _____ **Agadem** _____

   c. From Tripoli to Nguigmi is about _____ **2,200** _____ KM or _____ **1,350** _____ MI **All answers here are approximate.**

4. Find the distance between the following cities and the direction from the
   first city to the second.

	Distance		Direction
a. Casablanca to Marrakech	about 300 KM	about 200 MI	SW or S
b. Nouakchott to Tunis	about 3,700 KM	about 2,300 MI	NE
c. Dakar to Cairo	about 5,900 KM	about 3,600 MI	NE

5. How far are the ruins at Thebes from Cairo? _____ **about 400** KM _____ **about 300** MI

6. If a camel went 40 kilometers a day, how long would a trip by

   camel from Cairo to the ruins take? _____ **about 10 days** _____

Skill Check

Vocabulary Check map scale inset map miles (MI) kilometers (KM)

1. To show the relationship between the actual size of a place and its

   reduced size on a map, map makers use _____a map scale_____.

2. Distances in the United States are usually measured in ____miles (MI)____.

3. Distances in countries other than the United States are usually

   measured in _____kilometers (KM)_____.

Map Check

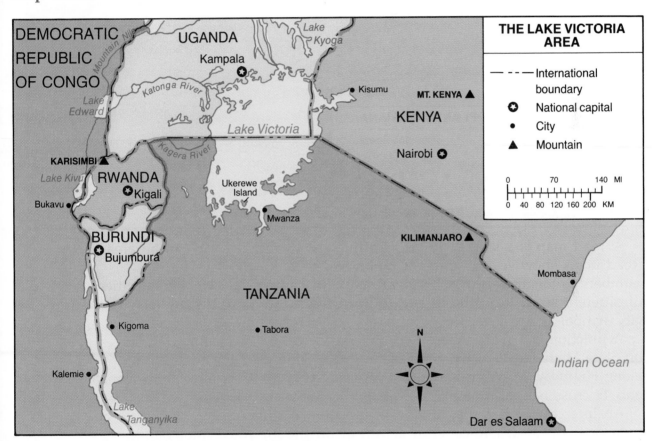

1. About how long is the border between Kenya and Tanzania?

   ___760___ KM ___460___ MI

   All answers here are approximate.

2. Find the distance between these places.

   a. Nairobi to Mombasa about 440 KM about 270 MI

   b. Dar es Salaam to Kigali about 1,150 KM about 710 MI

   c. Kampala to Bujumbura about 540 KM about 330 MI

   d. Mt. Kenya to Kilimanjaro about 330 KM about 200 MI

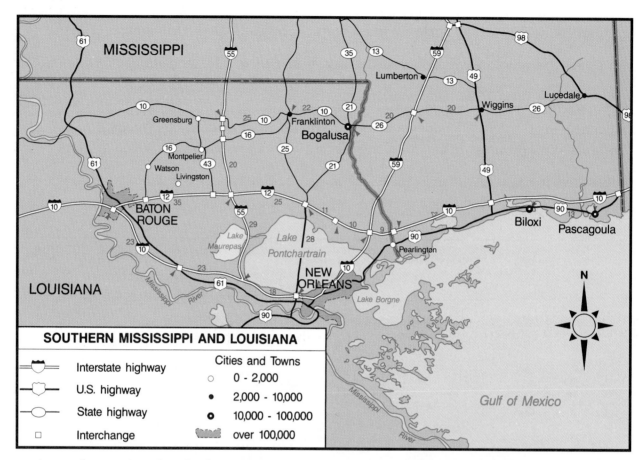

A road map is a kind of route map that shows the highways of an area. Road maps show several kinds of highways. Most major roads have numbers to identify them. This road map also has special symbols for cities of different sizes. Read the legend to learn the meaning of the highway and city symbols.

A **junction** is a place where two highways cross or meet. Put your finger on State Highway 26 at the right of the map. Slide your finger to the left along Highway 26. What is the first highway you cross? Where Highways 26 and 49 cross is a junction. **U.S. Highway 49**

An **interchange** is a special kind of junction. An interchange is a place on a major highway where cars can get on or off the highway. Interchanges have special connecting ramps to allow vehicles to change roads without interrupting the flow of traffic. Find an interchange on Interstate 12.

Find the red numbers on the map between junctions and cities. These **mileage markers** give the distance in miles between each set of red triangles. What is the distance between Biloxi and Pascagoula on U.S. 90? **13 miles**

► Which city is larger, Biloxi or Pearlington? **Biloxi**

► What body of water do Interstate 10 and Interstate 12 go around? **Lake Pontchartrain or Lake Maurepas**

► Where is the junction of State Highway 25 and State Highway 10? **Franklinton**

► If you got off Interstate 59 south of Lumberton, what highway would you be on? What is the first city you would come to going west? **State Hwy. 26 Bogalusa**

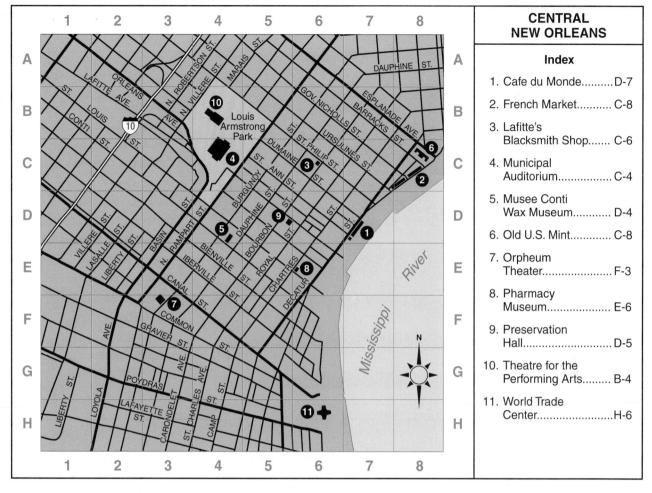

CENTRAL NEW ORLEANS

Index

1. Cafe du Monde..........D-7
2. French Market...........C-8
3. Lafitte's Blacksmith Shop.......C-6
4. Municipal Auditorium.................C-4
5. Musee Conti Wax Museum............D-4
6. Old U.S. Mint.............C-8
7. Orpheum Theater......................F-3
8. Pharmacy Museum...................E-6
9. Preservation Hall............................D-5
10. Theatre for the Performing Arts.........B-4
11. World Trade Center.......................H-6

A street map is also a route map.

Maps often have grids. A **grid** is a pattern of lines which cross to form squares on the map. With a grid, it is easy to find places on the map. Each square in the grid is labeled with a **coordinate**. The rows of squares are labeled with a letter. The columns are labeled with a number. Each individual square has coordinates of a letter and a number. The **map index** lists places alphabetically with their grid coordinates. If you know the name of a place, and you want to find it on the map, begin by looking in the index. Find the Pharmacy Museum in the index. What are the coordinates for the Pharmacy Museum? Now find the row labeled E on the map. Slide your finger across the row until you come to column 6. Find the Pharmacy Museum in that square.

► Find Louis Armstrong Park on the map. **Theatre for the Performing Arts,** What two buildings are located in this park? **Municipal Auditorium** What street borders the park on the east? **N. Rampart Street**

► Find Lafitte's Blacksmith Shop on the map. **Pharmacy Museum, World Trade Center** What other buildings are in that column?

► Use the map index and grid to find these places on the map.
   Cafe du Monde **D-7** Preservation Hall **D-5** Orpheum Theater **F-3**

► What places could you visit if you walked southwest on Decatur from the U.S. Mint? **French Market, Cafe du Monde, Pharmacy Museum**

Reading a Route Map

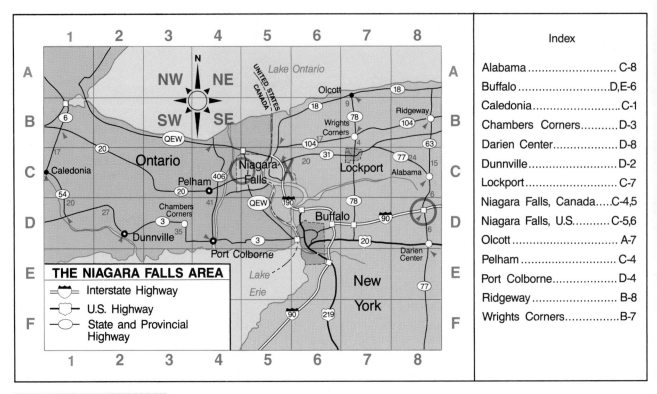

Index

Alabama C-8
Buffalo D,E-6
Caledonia.........................C-1
Chambers Corners...........D-3
Darien Center..................D-8
Dunnville.........................D-2
Lockport..........................C-7
Niagara Falls, Canada.....C-4,5
Niagara Falls, U.S...........C-5,6
Olcott A-7
Pelham C-4
Port Colborne..................D-4
Ridgeway B-8
Wrights Corners...............B-7

MAP ATTACK!

- **Read the title.** This map shows ___the Niagara Falls area___.
- **Read the compass rose.** Label the intermediate direction arrows.
- **Read the grid and index.** Finish labeling the grid rows and columns.

1. Put an X on Niagara Falls, U.S.A. Put an O on Niagara Falls, Canada.

2. What highway enters Niagara Falls, U.S.A., from the north? ___18___

3. If you left State Highway 20 at the first junction out of Niagara Falls and drove south, what city would you come to? ___Port Colborne___

4. a. What highway goes along the north shore of Lake Erie?___3___

   b. In what city could you turn north to Lake Ontario? ___Port Colborne___

5. Circle the interchange on Interstate 90 just south of Alabama. If you exited I-90 at that interchange and drove north 21 miles, what city would you come to? ___Ridgeway___

6. What highways form a junction at Ridgeway? ___63 and 104___

7. Where would you see this sign?

Niagara Falls	20
Wrights Corners	4
Alabama	24

___in Lockport___

Reading a Route Map

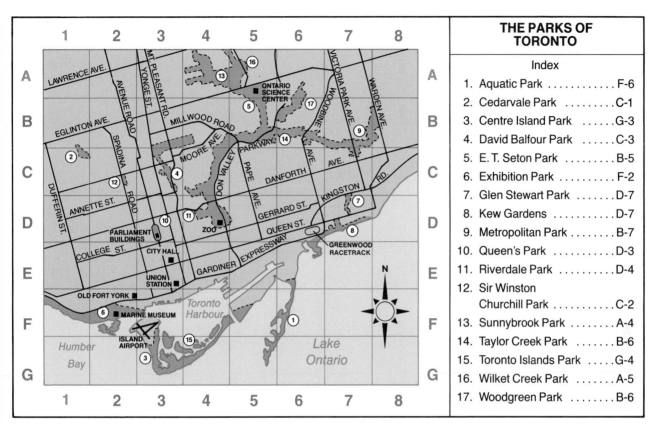

THE PARKS OF TORONTO

Index

1. Aquatic Park F-6
2. Cedarvale Park C-1
3. Centre Island Park G-3
4. David Balfour Park C-3
5. E. T. Seton Park B-5
6. Exhibition Park F-2
7. Glen Stewart Park D-7
8. Kew Gardens D-7
9. Metropolitan Park B-7
10. Queen's Park D-3
11. Riverdale Park D-4
12. Sir Winston
    Churchill Park C-2
13. Sunnybrook Park A-4
14. Taylor Creek Park B-6
15. Toronto Islands Park G-4
16. Wilket Creek Park A-5
17. Woodgreen Park B-6

1. Complete the grid by adding the missing letters and numbers.
2. Name each park described.

   a. just south of Wilket Creek Park _____E.T. Seton Park_____

   b. in the same grid square as Woodgreen Park ___Taylor Creek Park___

   c. with the Parliament buildings _____Queen's Park_____

   d. at the corner of Moore Avenue and Spadina Road

   _____Sir Winston Churchill Park_____

   e. on the southern end of Woodbine Avenue ___Kew Gardens___

3. What two parks are on the same island as the Island Airport?

   Centre Island Park and Toronto Islands Park

4. What parks border the Don Valley Parkway? _____

   Riverdale Park, Taylor Creek Park, Woodgreen Park, E. T. Seton Park

5. What street is east of Metropolitan Park?

   Warden Avenue

6. What streets would take you from Woodgreen Park to Sir Winston

   Churchill Park? _____Answers will vary._____

Reading a Route Map

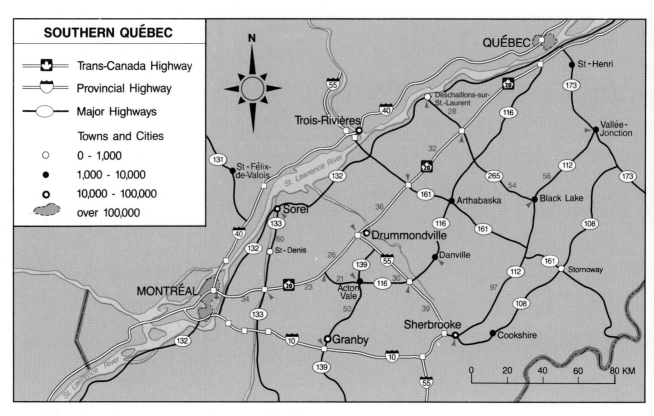

1. What highway takes you from Granby to Acton Vale? _____139_____

2. a. How many kilometers is it from Acton Vale to the interchange just
   south of Granby? (Read the mileage marker.) _____50_____

   b. Use the map scale to measure the distance "as the crow flies"
   (in a straight line) from Acton Vale to the interchange just south of
   Granby. The distance is ___about 45___ kilometers.

   c. Why do you think the distances differ? ___The highway curves.___

3. a. What is the distance "as the crow flies" from the interchange on
   Highway 55 southeast of Drummondville to Granby? _about 55 kilometers_

   b. What is the distance along the highways? ___80 kilometers___

4. a. Where is the junction of Highways 112 and 265? ___Black Lake___

   b. If you drove 54 kilometers northwest of that junction, what junction
   would you come to? _____20 and 265_____

5. a. What highway goes along the southern shore of the St. Lawrence River?

   _____132_____

   b. Where would you exit that highway to get to Black Lake?

   ___Answers will vary.___

Skill Check

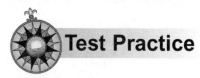

Test Practice

Vocabulary Check

      junction   interchange   grid
      coordinate   mileage marker   index

Write the word or phrase that best completes each sentence.

1. A _____junction_____ is the place where two roads meet or cross.

2. An _____interchange_____ is a junction of major highways and has special connecting ramps or roads.

3. A _____mileage marker_____ indicates distance between cities.

Map Check

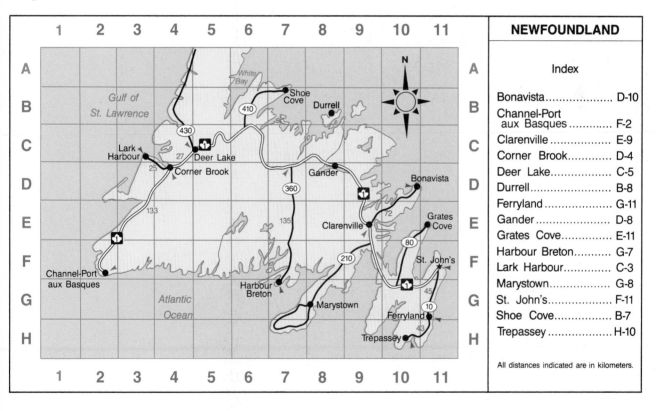

1. Complete the map grid by adding the missing letters and numbers.
2. Name each place described below.

    a. a city at the junction of Highways 1 and 430 _____Deer Lake_____

    b. a city 88 kilometers south of St. John's _____Trepassey_____

    c. a city 25 kilometers northwest of Corner Brook _____Lark Harbour_____

3. Where do you leave Highway 1 to go to Bonavista? _____at Clarenville_____
4. Which highways would take you from Harbour Breton to Shoe Cove?

                360, 1, 410

Geography Themes Up Close

Place focuses on the physical and human features of an area. Is the climate humid and wet or cold and dry? Are there mountains, hills, lakes, or rivers? How are the people governed? What language do they speak? The answers to these kinds of questions describe place.

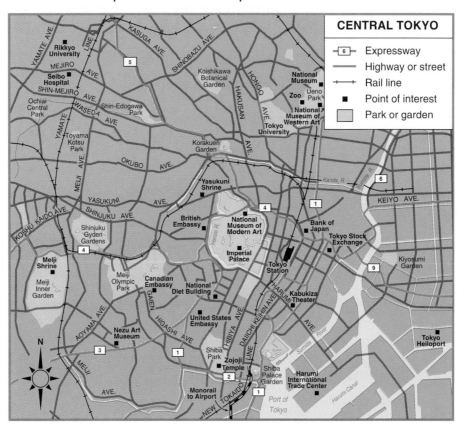

1. Based on the map, what are two physical and two human features of Tokyo?

   Physical features: Kanda River, Sumida River, Port of Tokyo; Human features: parks, gardens, government buildings, shrines, stock exchange, temples, museums, banks, universities, roads, and theaters

2. Name a human feature that is in Tokyo because Tokyo is the national capital.

   Imperial Palace, National Diet Building, foreign embassies, national library

3. How do the features of Tokyo differ from those in your town or city?

   Answers will vary, but should offer some features from the student's town or city.

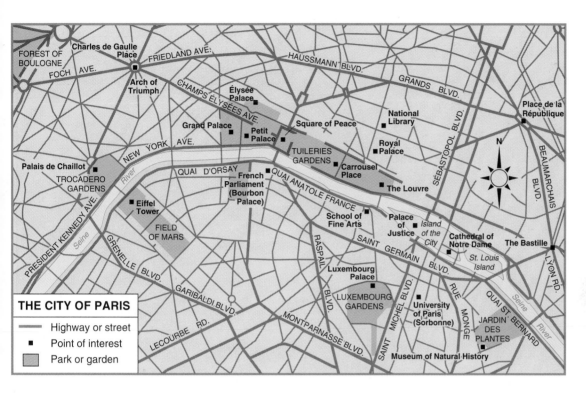

The City of Paris

THE CITY OF PARIS

— Highway or street
■ Point of interest
▨ Park or garden

4. Based on the map, name a physical feature of Paris.

   Seine River, Island of the City, or St. Louis Island

5. Name three human features of Paris other than buildings.

   Any three human features, other than buildings, shown on the map

6. How do the features of Paris differ from those of Tokyo?

   Answers will vary, but should offer examples based on the two maps.

7. What are two famous buildings in Paris shown on the map?

   Answers should include two of the following: Eiffel Tower, Cathedral of

   Notre Dame, the Louvre, Arch of Triumph, or other famous buildings.

Relief and Elevation

By reading a **relief map** you can learn something about the physical features of a place. The map on this page is a relief map of Russia. Russia is now an independent country. It was formerly part of the Union of Soviet Socialist Republics.

Shading on relief maps shows the shape and height of the land. The highest, steepest mountain ranges have dark shading. Lower, less steep mountain ranges have lighter shading. Valleys and plains have no shading.

Besides mountains, relief maps usually show the major rivers of a place. A river's **source** is where it begins. A river flows downhill towards its **mouth**, where it empties into a sea or ocean. Many rivers flow into other rivers. These smaller rivers are called **tributaries**.

► Name a tributary of the Lena River. **Vilyuy River**

► Name three rivers that flow north. **Ob River, Yenisey River, Lena River**

► Does the Ob River flow mainly through low lands or high lands? **low lands**

► In which mountain range are the sources of the Ural and Volga Rivers? **Ural Mountains** These rivers empty into what sea? **Caspian Sea**

► What is the longest mountain range in Russia? **Ural Mountains**

► What other landforms are shown on this map? **peninsulas, plains, islands, plateau**

► What other water forms are shown on this map? **gulfs, oceans, seas, lakes, strait**

► What mountain on this map is 10,325 feet high? **Mt. Pobeda**

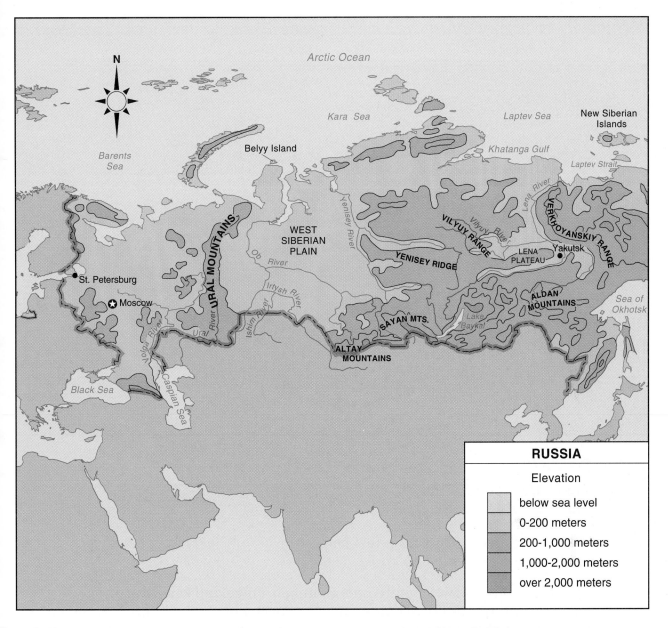

This map shows part of Russia. Colors on the map show how high the land is, or its elevation. **Elevation** is the height of the land above or below the level of the sea. Read the legend to understand what elevation each color represents.

► What color shows the highest areas in Russia? **purple or dark blue**

► What color shows the lowest areas? **yellow**

Like a relief map, an elevation map gives a picture of how the land looks. An elevation map uses zones of color to show areas of land with similar elevation. A relief map gives an almost three-dimensional picture of the land. In what ways might we use relief and elevation maps? **to visualize the way the land looks and to tell its elevation**

► These places are in which elevation zones?

Moscow	Lake Baykal	Yakutsk
0–200 meters	1,000–2,000 meters	0–200 meters

► At what elevation is the source of the Ural River? **200–1,000 meters**

► Where in Russia is the elevation lowest? **near the Caspian Sea**

Reading a Relief Map

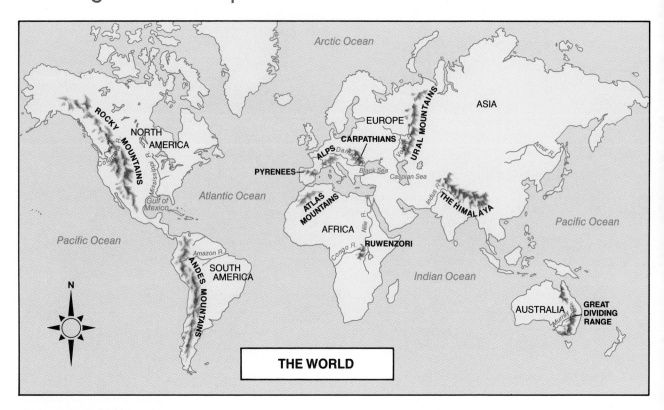

Arctic Ocean

ASIA

EUROPE

ROCKY MOUNTAINS

NORTH AMERICA

CARPATHIANS

URAL MOUNTAINS

ALPS

Danube

PYRENEES

Black Sea

Caspian Sea

Columbia

Mississippi

Atlantic Ocean

Gulf of Mexico

ATLAS MOUNTAINS

Indus R.

THE HIMALAYA

Pacific Ocean

Nile R.

AFRICA

RUWENZORI

Pacific Ocean

Amazon R.

Congo R.

Indian Ocean

ANDES MOUNTAINS

SOUTH AMERICA

N

AUSTRALIA

GREAT DIVIDING RANGE

Murray

THE WORLD

MAP ATTACK!

● **Read the title.** This map shows _____the world_____.

What is one thing to learn from this map? **Answers will vary.**

1. Complete the chart below. Identify one mountain range and one river in each continent. Write the direction each river flows and the body of water into which it empties.

Continent	Mountain Range	River	Direction	Body of Water
a. North America	Rocky Mountains	Columbia / Mississippi	southwest / south	Pacific Ocean / Gulf of Mexico
b. South America	Andes Mountains	Amazon	east	Atlantic Ocean
c. Asia	Urals / The Himalaya	Amur / Indus	east / northwest, southwest	Pacific Ocean / Indian Ocean
d. Europe	Carpathians Urals / Pyrenees Alps	Danube / Volga	east / south	Black Sea / Caspian Sea
e. Australia	Great Dividing Range	Murray	southwest	Indian Ocean

2. Draw a conclusion. Rivers may flow north, south, east, or west. What determines the direction that a river flows?

the elevation

Reading an Elevation Map

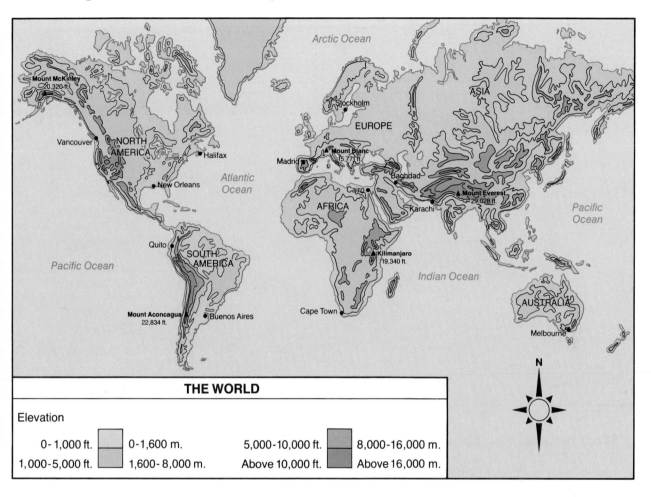

THE WORLD

Elevation

0- 1,000 ft.	0-1,600 m.	5,000-10,000 ft.	8,000-16,000 m.
1,000-5,000 ft.	1,600- 8,000 m.	Above 10,000 ft.	Above 16,000 m.

1. Circle the places in this list that are between 0 and 1,000 feet above sea level.

   (New Orleans)   Baghdad   Madrid   (Cairo)   (Cape Town)

   (Karachi)   (Stockholm)   (Buenos Aires)   (Melbourne)

2. Write the elevation and continent of these mountain peaks.

Mountain	Elevation	Continent
a. Aconcagua	22,834 ft.	South America
b. Blanc	15,771 ft.	Europe
c. Everest	29,028 ft.	Asia
d. McKinley	20,320 ft.	North America
e. Kilimanjaro	19,340 ft.	Africa

3. Draw a conclusion. The largest area of land more than 10,000 feet above sea level is on which continent? ___Asia___

Reading a Map of Turkey

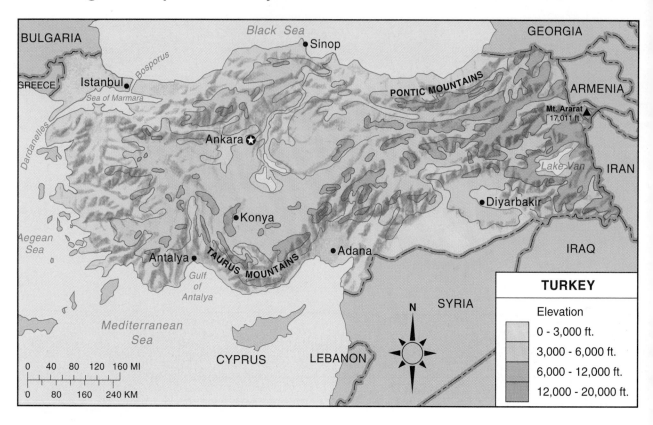

1. What mountain is shown on this map? _____Mt. Ararat_____

   How high is this mountain? _____17,011 feet_____

2. Identify the two mountain ranges shown on the map. For each one, identify the part of the country in which it is located.

Mountain Range	Part of Country
a. _____Pontic Mountains_____	_____northeast_____
b. _____Taurus Mountains_____	_____south_____

3. Is the eastern or western part of Turkey more mountainous? _eastern_

4. Does the elevation of the land increase or decrease as it approaches the

   coast? _____decrease_____

5. About how far from Istanbul is Mt. Ararat? _____about 800 miles_____

6. About how far from Sinop is Adana? _____about 350 miles_____

7. Imagine you are traveling by boat from Antalya in southern Turkey to Sinop in northern Turkey. List the bodies of water you must cross.

   Gulf of Antalya, Mediterranean Sea, Aegean Sea, Dardanelles,

   Sea of Marmara, Bosporus, Black Sea.

Skill Check

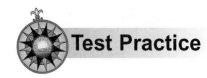

Vocabulary Check   relief   elevation   mouth
                         tributaries   source

Write the word that best completes each sentence.

1. A(n) _____relief_____ map uses shading to show mountains on a map.

2. A(n) ____elevation____ map uses zones of color to show the height of land.

3. A river's ___source___ is where it begins, and its ___mouth___ is where it empties into a sea or ocean.

4. Rivers that flow into a larger river are _____tributaries_____ .

Map Check

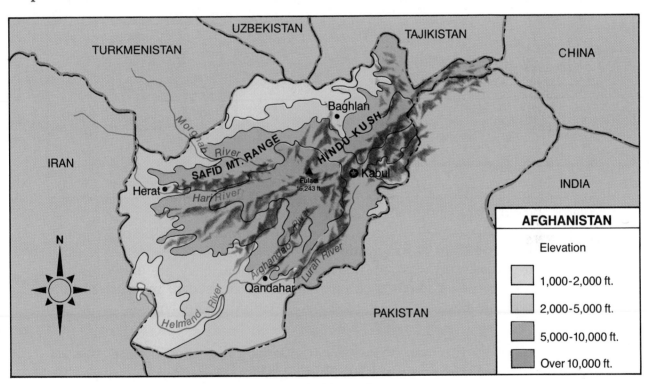

1. Name two tributaries of the Helmand River.

   Arghandab River, Lurah River

2. Name a river that flows through the Safid Mt. Range.

   Hari River or Morghab River

3. Name a river whose source is in the Hindu Kush Mountains.

   Helmand River, Arghandab River, Lurah River

4. Where are the areas of lowest elevation in Afghanistan?

   in the far north and the far southwest

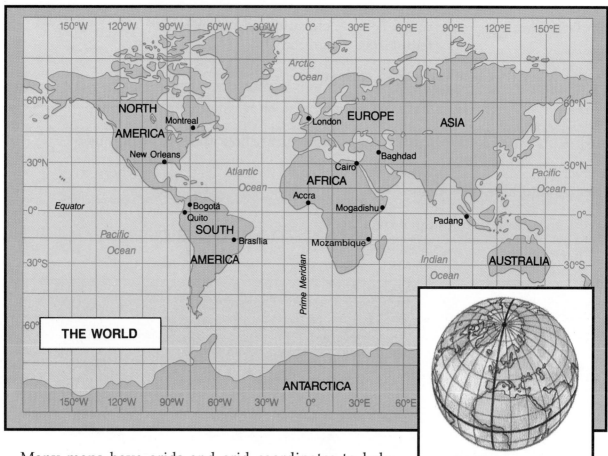

150°W 120°W 90°W 60°W 30°W 0° 30°E 60°E 90°E 120°E 150°E

Arctic Ocean

60°N

NORTH AMERICA
Montreal
New Orleans

EUROPE
London
ASIA

Baghdad
Cairo
AFRICA
Accra
Mogadishu

60°N

30°N

Atlantic Ocean

Pacific Ocean

30°N

Equator
0°

Bogotá
Quito
SOUTH
Brasília
AMERICA

Mozambique

Padang

0°

Pacific Ocean

Prime Meridian

Indian Ocean

AUSTRALIA

30°S

30°S

60°

THE WORLD

ANTARCTICA

150°W 120°W 90°W 60°W 30°W 0° 30°E 60°E

Many maps have grids and grid coordinates to help locate places. World maps and globes have grids on them. Look at the world map above. The grid pattern on the map is made up of lines of **latitude** and lines of **longitude**.

The lines that go east and west are the lines of latitude. They are also called **parallels** because they never touch each other. Latitude is used to measure distances north and south of the Equator. The Equator is 0° latitude. The symbol ° stands for **degrees**.

► Find the Equator on the map above. What cities lie near the Equator? **Quito, Bogotá, Accra, Mogadishu, Padang** Look north of the Equator to find 30° North latitude. What cities lie near 30° North latitude? Find 15° South latitude. What cities lie near 15° South latitude? **30°N: New Orleans, Cairo, Baghdad; 15°S: Brasília, Mozambique**

The lines that go north and south are the lines of longitude. They are also called **meridians**. Longitude is used to measure distances east and west of the **Prime Meridian**. The Prime Meridian is 0° longitude and goes from the North Pole to the South Pole. All lines of longitude meet at the North and South Poles.

► Find the Prime Meridian at 0° longitude. What cities lie near the Prime Meridian? Now look east of the Prime Meridian to find 45° East longitude. What cities lie near 45° East longitude? Find 75° West longitude. What cities lie near 75° West longitude? **0°: London, Accra; 45°E: Baghdad, Mogadishu; 75°W: Montreal, Bogotá, Quito**

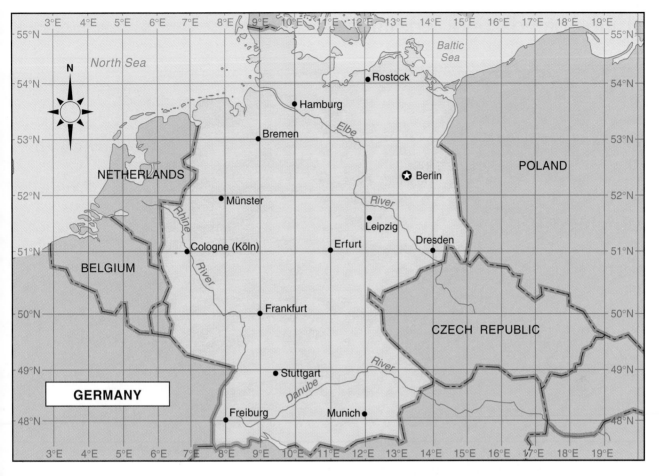

Look at the map of the world on page 42. You can see that the lines of latitude begin with 0° at the Equator and increase as they go north and south. The highest numbers are at the poles. The North Pole is 90° North latitude, and the South Pole is 90° South latitude.

The lines of longitude begin with 0° at the Prime Meridian and increase as they go east and west of the Prime Meridian. The highest number is 180°. The line of longitude directly opposite the Prime Meridian is 180°.

The lines of latitude and longitude form a grid pattern. This grid enables us to locate every place on Earth. Look at the map above. Find 51° North latitude. Run your finger along it until it crosses 7° East longitude. You have found the city of Cologne. The coordinates of Cologne are 51° North latitude and 7° East longitude, or 51°N, 7°E. Every spot on Earth has its own coordinates.

▶ Use latitude and longitude coordinates to find these places on the map. The coordinate for latitude is always named first.

Frankfurt	50°N, 9°E
Bremen	53°N, 9°E
Munich	48°N, 12°E

▶ Estimate the coordinates (latitude and longitude) of these places on the map:

Münster	**52°N, 8°E**
Leipzig	**51°N, 12°E**
Stuttgart	**49°N, 9°E**

Using Latitude and Longitude

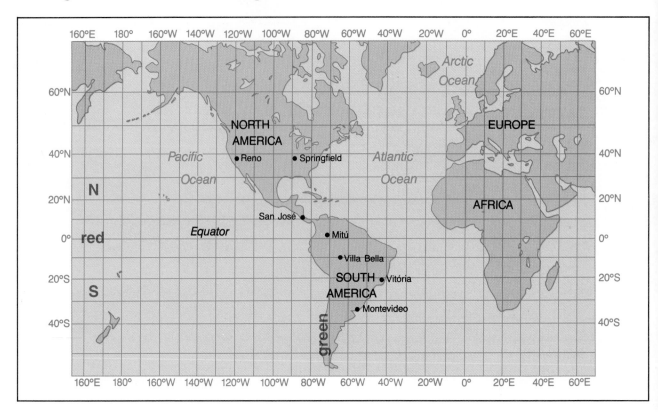

1. Trace the 70° W meridian in green.

   a. Is that line east or west of the Prime Meridian? _____ west _____
   b. Is most of the area shown on the map in the Eastern or Western

      Hemisphere? _____ the Western Hemisphere _____

2. Trace the Equator in red.
   Draw an N just north of the Equator.
   Draw an S just south of the Equator.

3. a. What city is near the place where the Equator and 70°W cross?

      _____ Mitú _____

   b. What are its coordinates? _____ 0° _____, 70°W.

4. Find the missing coordinate for these cities.

   a. Springfield   40°N , __ 90°W __

   b. Vitória   __ 20°S __,   40°W

   c. Reno   __ 40°N __,   120°W

   d. San José   10°N , __ 85°W __

   e. Villa Bella   __ 10°S __,   65°W

   f. Montevideo   35°S , __ 55°W __

Using Latitude and Longitude

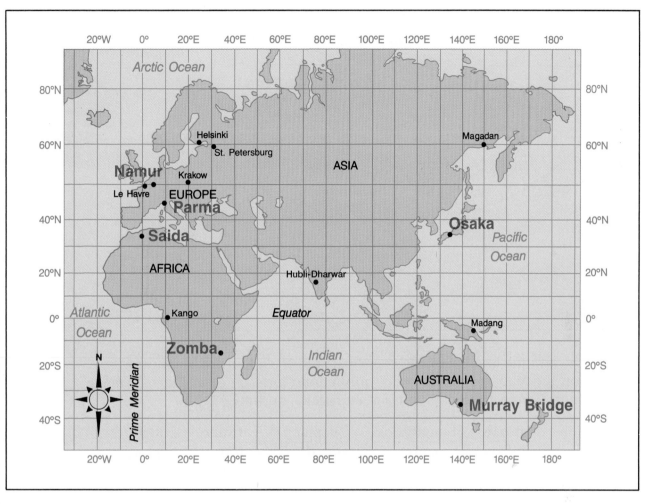

1. Label the cities at these locations on the map.
   a. 35° S, 140°E   Murray Bridge
   b. 50°N,   5°E   Namur
   c. 35°N, 135°E   Osaka
   d. 45°N, 10°E   Parma
   e. 15° S, 35°E   Zomba
   f. 35°N,   0°   Saida

2. Write the latitude and longitude coordinates of these cities.

	Latitude	Longitude
a. Helsinki	60°N	25°E
b. Le Havre	50°N	0°
c. St. Petersburg	60°N	30°E
d. Madang	5°S	145°E
e. Krakow	50°N	20°E
f. Hubli-Dharwar	15°N	75°E

Tracking a Hurricane

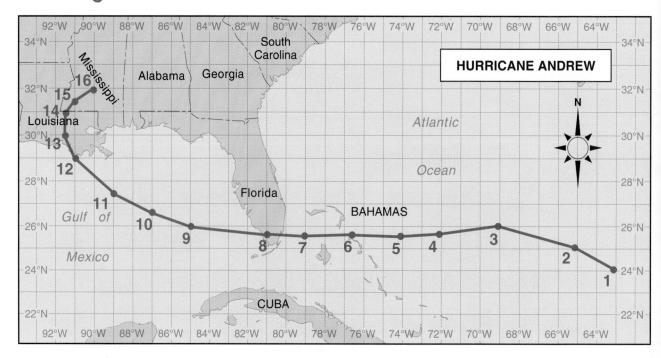

1. Use the latitude and longitude coordinates to track Hurricane Andrew's path on the map above. Put a dot on the map for each coordinate. Number each dot. Connect the dots to track Hurricane Andrew's path.

Position	Latitude	Longitude	Position	Latitude	Longitude
1	24°N	63°W	9	26°N	85°W
2	25°N	65°W	10	26½°N	87°W
3	26°N	69°W	11	27½°N	89°W
4	25½°N	72°W	12	29°N	91°W
5	25½°N	74°W	13	30°N	91½°W
6	25½°N	76½°W	14	31°N	91½°W
7	25½°N	79°W	15	31½°N	91°W
8	25½°N	81°W	16	32°N	90°W

2. Write the direction that Hurricane Andrew traveled

   a. from Position 1 to Position 3. _____ NW _____

   b. from Position 4 to Position 8. _____ W _____

   c. from Position 9 to Position 13. _____ NW _____

   d. from Position 14 to Position 16. _____ NE _____

3. In what body of water did the hurricane begin? _____ Atlantic Ocean _____

4. What other body of water did it cross? _____ Gulf of Mexico _____

5. Where did Hurricane Andrew hit land?

   _____ Bahamas, Florida, and Louisiana _____

Skill Check

Vocabulary Check

latitude	degrees	longitude
meridians	parallels	Prime Meridian

Write the word or phrase that best completes each sentence.

1. The _____ **Prime Meridian** _____ is the starting point for measuring distances east and west.

2. Lines of latitude, also called _____ **parallels** _____, measure distances north and south of the Equator.

3. Lines of longitude, also called _____ **meridians** _____, meet at the poles.

Map Check

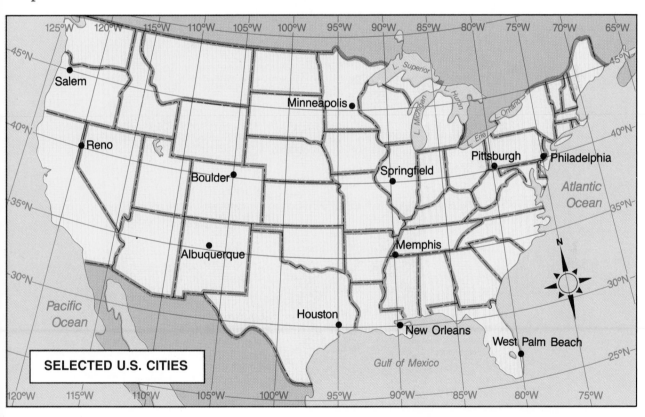

SELECTED U.S. CITIES

1. Name the cities at these locations.

   a. 40°N, 90°W _____ **Springfield** _____ c. 40°N, 105°W _____ **Boulder** _____

   b. 40°N, 75°W _____ **Philadelphia** _____ d. 35°N, 90°W _____ **Memphis** _____

2. Write the latitude and longitude coordinates of these cities.

	Latitude	Longitude			Latitude	Longitude
a. New Orleans	30°N	90°W		c. Reno	40°N	120°W
b. Pittsburgh	40°N	80°W		d. Houston	30°N	95°W

Geography Themes Up Close

Location describes where a place is found. Every place on Earth has a location. There are two ways to describe location. **Relative location** describes a place by what it is near or what is around it. **Absolute location** is the specific address or latitude and longitude coordinates of a place. For example, the postal address of your home is an absolute location.

SOUTH AMERICA

- - - International boundary
⊛ Capital City

1. Venezuela is in the northern part of South America. This country is located along the Caribbean Sea. Label Venezuela on the map.

2. This South American country is found in the central part of the continent. It is southeast of Peru and north of Argentina. Write the name of the country here and then label it on the map.

   Bolivia

3. Label these national capitals on the map.
   a. Lima 12°S, 77°W
   b. Cayenne 5°N, 52°W

4. Mount Aconcagua's absolute location is 33°S, 70°W. Circle Mount Aconcagua on the map.

5. Name the cities found at these locations:
   a. 5°N, 75°W _____**Bogotá**_____   c. 26°S, 58°W_____**Asunción**_____

   b. 19°S, 65°W _____**Sucre**_____   d. 6°N, 55°W _____**Paramaribo**_____

6. Find the Amazon River. Describe its relative location.

   Answers will vary, but may include that the Amazon River is located in

   northern Brazil, from the Atlantic Ocean west to the Andes Mountains.

7. What is the absolute location of the Mato Grosso Plateau?

   14°S, 56°W

8. Name the country located at 33°S, 55°W.

   Uruguay

9. Give the absolute location of Brasília, Brazil.

   16°S, 48°W

10. Describe the relative location of the country of Guyana.

    Answers will vary, but may include that Guyana is located in northern

    South America. It is north of Brazil, east of Venezuela, west of

    Suriname, and south of the Caribbean Sea.

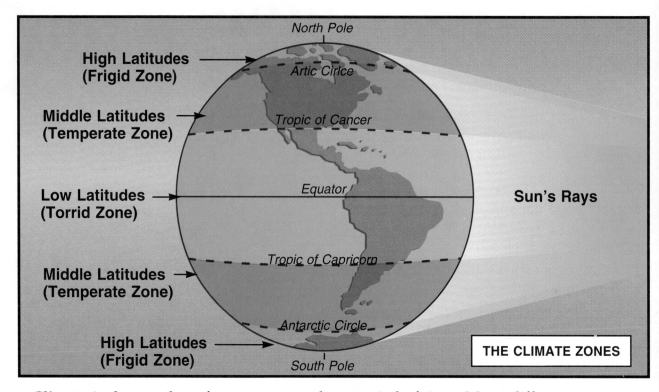

High Latitudes (Frigid Zone) — North Pole — Artic Cirlce

Middle Latitudes (Temperate Zone) — Tropic of Cancer

Low Latitudes (Torrid Zone) — Equator — Sun's Rays

Middle Latitudes (Temperate Zone) — Tropic of Capricorn

High Latitudes (Frigid Zone) — Antarctic Circle — South Pole

THE CLIMATE ZONES

Climate is the weather of an area over a long period of time. Many different factors determine what kind of climate a place has. Some factors include elevation, winds, and whether the place is near water.

One of the most important factors in determining climate is how directly the rays of the sun hit the place. Because Earth is round, the sun's rays do not hit it evenly. In places near the Equator, the sun is directly overhead. These places receive direct rays. In places near the poles, the sun is low in the sky. These places receive slanted rays. The direct rays give more heat. The slanted rays give less heat.

The world can be divided into **climate zones** based on how directly the sun's rays strike Earth. Look at the map above to find the climate zones.

> The **low latitudes**, or **Torrid Zone**, is the area between the Tropic of Cancer (23½°N) and the Tropic of Capricorn (23½°S). *Torrid* means "very hot." The sun's direct rays heat the Torrid Zone all year round.
>
> The **high latitudes**, or **Frigid Zones**, cover the area between the Arctic Circle (66½°N) and the North Pole (90°N) and the area between the Antarctic Circle (66½°S) and the South Pole (90°S). *Frigid* means "very cold." The sun is low in the sky in these areas, so only slanted rays hit them. As a result, these zones are cold all year.
>
> The **middle latitudes**, or **Temperate Zones**, are between the Torrid Zone and the Frigid Zones. *Temperate* means "balanced." The climate in the Temperate Zones is a balance between the heat of the Torrid Zone and the cold of the Frigid Zones. The climate of places in the Temperate Zones changes from season to season.

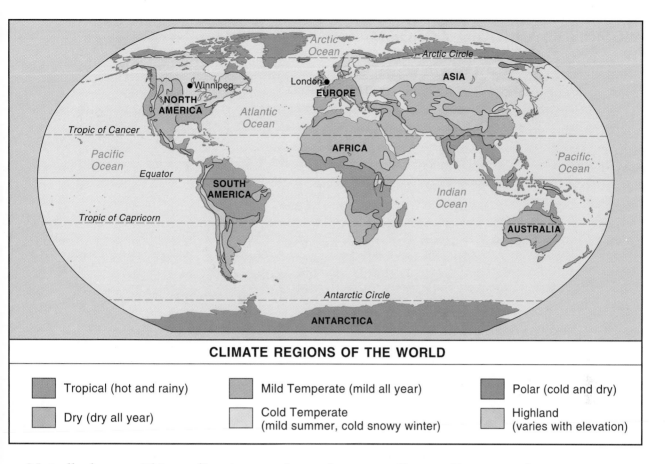

CLIMATE REGIONS OF THE WORLD

Tropical (hot and rainy)	Mild Temperate (mild all year)	Polar (cold and dry)
Dry (dry all year)	Cold Temperate (mild summer, cold snowy winter)	Highland (varies with elevation)

Not all places within a climate zone have the same climate. For example, Winnipeg, Canada, and London, England, are both in the Temperate Zone. The rays of sunlight that strike Winnipeg are about as direct as the ones that strike London. Yet the two places have very different climates. London has a much warmer climate because it is near the sea. This is an example of how factors other than sunlight affect the climate of a place.

To reflect differences within climate zones, a list of **climate regions** has been developed. There are six basic climate regions. As you read about the climate regions of the world, locate them on the map above.

The **tropical climate** is hot and rainy. Much of the world's rain forests and jungles grow in tropical climates.

Areas that have a **dry climate** are dry all year round. Much of the western United States has a dry climate. So does northern Africa, where the great Sahara desert is.

The **mild temperate climate** is mild all year.

Areas with **cold temperate climates** have mild summers, but the winters are cold and snowy.

Areas with a **polar climate** are cold and dry.

▶ Find the polar climates on the map. Why do you think this climate has the name it does? **because it is found near the poles**

Mountainous areas have a **highland climate**, which varies with the elevation.

Every place on Earth has one of these six climate regions. Find where you live on the map. In which climate region do you live? **Answers will depend on the students' location.**

Mastering Climate Zones

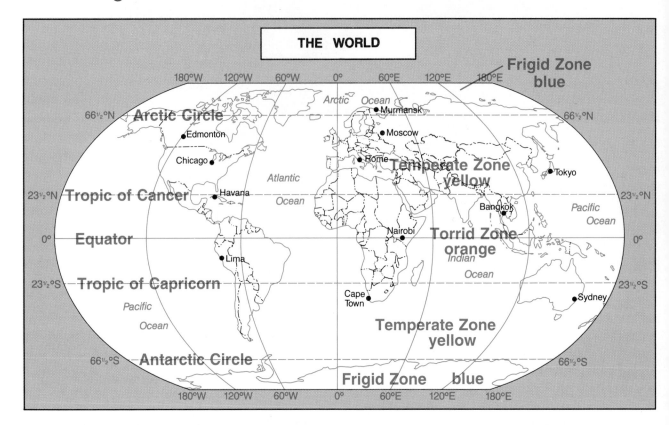

THE WORLD

1. Label the following places on the map. Write two labels twice.

Equator	Tropic of Cancer	Arctic Circle	Frigid Zone
Antarctic Circle	Tropic of Capricorn	Torrid Zone	Temperate Zone

2. Lightly color the Torrid Zone orange, the Temperate Zones yellow, and the Frigid Zones blue.

3. After each city below, write its climate zone. Then write whether it is in the high, middle, or low latitudes.

Place	Climate Zone	Latitudes
a. Murmansk	Frigid Zone	high
b. Chicago	Temperate Zone	middle
c. Cape Town	Temperate Zone	middle
d. Nairobi	Torrid Zone	low
e. Tokyo	Temperate Zone	middle
f. Havana	Torrid Zone	low
g. Rome	Temperate Zone	middle
h. Bangkok	Torrid Zone	low
i. Lima	Torrid Zone	low

Reading a Climate Map

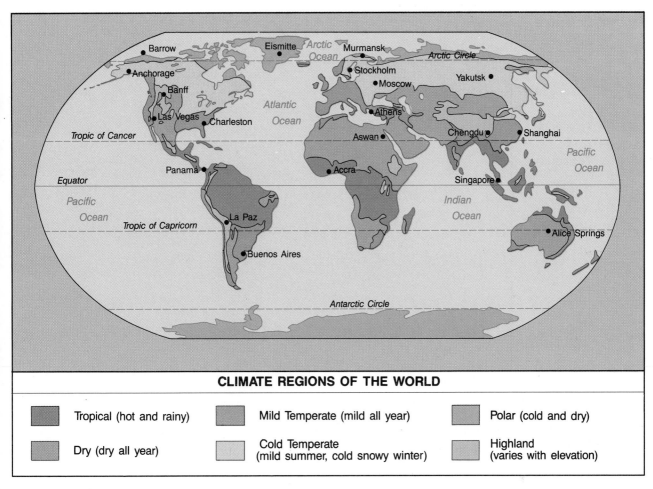

CLIMATE REGIONS OF THE WORLD

▮ Tropical (hot and rainy)	
▮ Dry (dry all year)	
▮ Mild Temperate (mild all year)	
▮ Cold Temperate (mild summer, cold snowy winter)	
▮ Polar (cold and dry)	
▮ Highland (varies with elevation)	

This map shows six climate regions of the world.

Write the name of three cities in each climate region.

1. Tropical   Singapore   Panamá   Accra

2. Dry   Las Vegas   Aswan   Alice Springs

3. Mild Temperate   Buenos Aires   Charleston   Athens   Shanghai

4. Cold Temperate   Anchorage   Stockholm   Moscow   Yakutsk

5. Polar   Barrow   Eismitte   Murmansk

6. Highland   Chengdu   La Paz   Banff

7. Which climate is found mostly in the Frigid Zone? _____ Polar _____

8. The tropical region is found mostly in what climate zone? _____ Torrid Zone _____

9. Draw a conclusion. Which has the most areas with cold snowy winters, the Northern or the Southern Hemisphere?

    The Northern Hemisphere

Reading a Climate Map of Europe

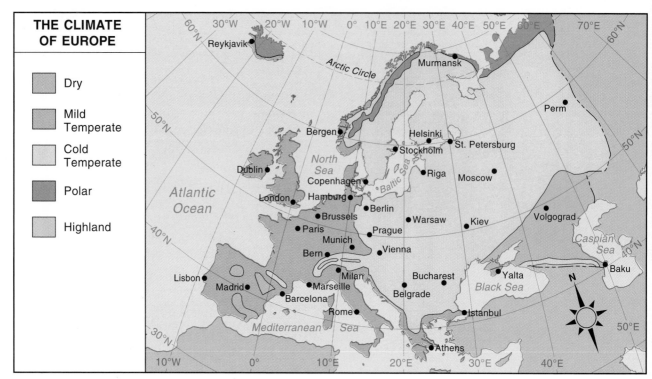

THE CLIMATE OF EUROPE

Dry

Mild Temperate

Cold Temperate

Polar

Highland

1. This map shows _____ **the climate of Europe** _____.

2. What type of climate does most of Europe have? _____ **cold temperate** _____

3. Name the cities at these locations. Then write the climate region.

   a. 60°N, 25°E   **Helsinki**   **cold temperate**

   b. 50°N, 45°E   **Volgograd**   **dry**

   c. 60°N, 5°E   **Bergen**   **mild temperate**

   d. 45°N, 20°E   **Belgrade**   **cold temperate**

   e. 55°N, 5°W   **Dublin**   **mild temperate**

4. Estimate the degrees latitude and longitude of each city. Then write its climate region.

	Latitude	Longitude	Climate Region
a. St. Petersburg	**60°N**	**30°E**	**cold temperate**
b. Kiev	**50°N**	**30°E**	**cold temperate**
c. London	**50°N**	**0°**	**mild temperate**
d. Baku	**40°N**	**50°E**	**dry**
e. Madrid	**40°N**	**5°W**	**mild temperate**

5. Polar regions on this map do not extend below what line of latitude? **60°N**

✓ Skill Check

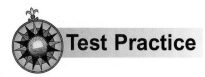

Vocabulary Check Torrid Zone   high latitudes   climate
Temperate Zone   middle latitudes
Frigid Zone   low latitudes

Write the word or phrase that best completes each sentence.

1. The Temperate Zone is found in the _____ middle latitudes _____ .
2. The area between the Tropic of Cancer and the Tropic of Capricorn

    is called the _____ low latitudes _____ , or _____ Torrid Zone _____ .
3. The high latitudes are also called the _____ Frigid Zone _____ .
4. The weather of an area over a long period of time is its _____ climate _____ .

Map Check

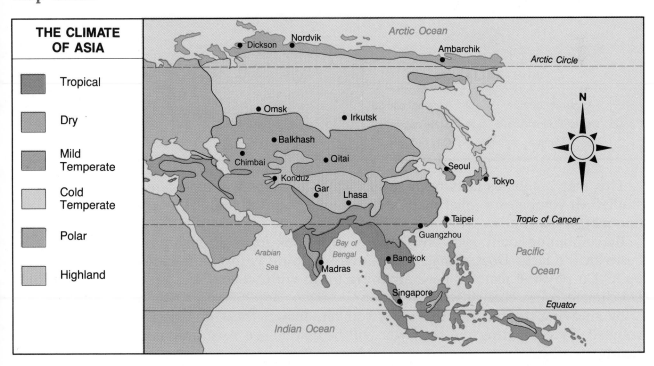

1. Write the names of three cities in each climate region.

    a. Tropical   Madras   Bangkok   Singapore

    b. Dry   Chimbai   Qitai   Balkhash

    c. Mild Temperate   Guangzhou   Taipei   Tokyo

    d. Cold Temperate   Omsk   Irkutsk   Seoul

    e. Polar   Dickson   Nordvik   Ambarchik

    f. Highland   Konduz   Gar   Lhasa

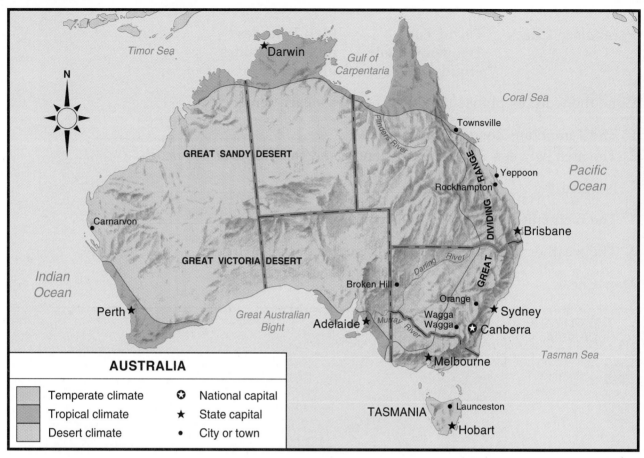

AUSTRALIA

▨ Temperate climate	✪ National capital
▨ Tropical climate	★ State capital
▨ Desert climate	• City or town

This map combines facts from several kinds of maps you have already studied. It combines a relief map, a climate map, and a political map into one map of Australia.

By combining many facts on a map, we can look for **relationships** between the facts. Does climate have anything to do with where cities are built? Do physical features have anything to do with where cities are built? Do climate zones change with elevation?

By studying the facts on this map, you can answer these questions for yourself. By comparing the facts you will be able to see Australia more clearly.

Read the Facts

► What and where are the seas, gulfs, and oceans that surround Australia?

north: Timor Sea, Gulf of Carpentaria, Coral Sea
south: Indian Ocean, Great Australian Bight, Tasman Sea
east: Pacific Ocean; west: Indian Ocean

► What and where are Australia's main mountain range and deserts? **Great Dividing Range: Great Sandy Desert: n Great Victoria Desert:**

► Where are Australia's temperate, tropical, and desert climates?

temperate: eastern and southeastern coast and Tasmania; tropical: northern and southern coasts; desert: central and northwestern and southern coasts

Draw Conclusions

► In what climate zone are most of Australia's cities? **temperate**

► Near what physical features are most of Australia's cities? **Great Dividing Range, and along the coasts**

► Where in Australia do very few people live? **in the desert**
Why do few people live there? **The climate is harsh.**

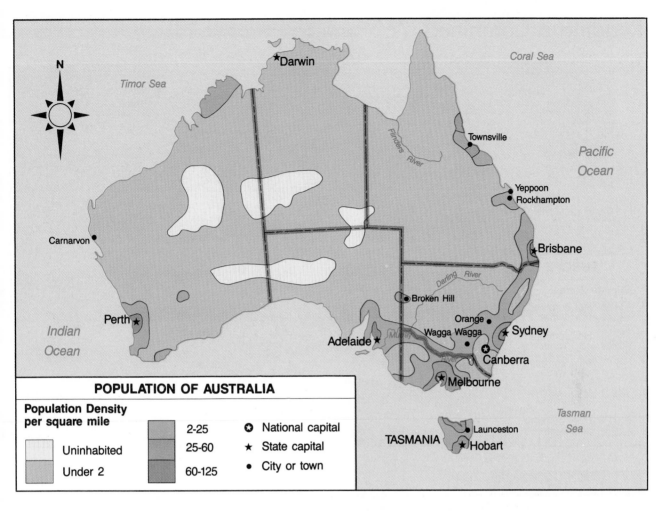

POPULATION OF AUSTRALIA

Population Density per square mile

Uninhabited

Under 2

2-25

25-60

60-125

⊘ National capital

★ State capital

• City or town

The map on this page shows Australia's population density. **Population density** is how many people live in a square mile. Parts of Australia are uninhabited, no one lives there. The darkest colors on the map stand for the places with the densest (most crowded) population. Find the area around Sydney, Australia's biggest city.

Read the key to learn what the purple color stands for. Closest to Sydney there are between 60 and 125 people living in each square mile. Point to Sydney, then move your finger inland (west or northwest). As you move away from the main part of the city, the population becomes less and less dense.

Read the Facts

► What are the five most densely populated places in Australia? Brisbane, Sydney, Melbourne, Adelaide, Perth

Compare the Maps Compare the facts on the map on this page and the map on page 56 to answer the questions.

► What is the population density in Australia's desert regions? uninhabited or under 2 per square mile

► What is the population density in the mountain region? from 2 to 125 per square mile

► What is the population density in the regions with mild temperate climates? from under 2 to 125 per square mile

Draw a Conclusion

► On the whole, which climate does Australia's population prefer? temperate

Reading a Combined Map

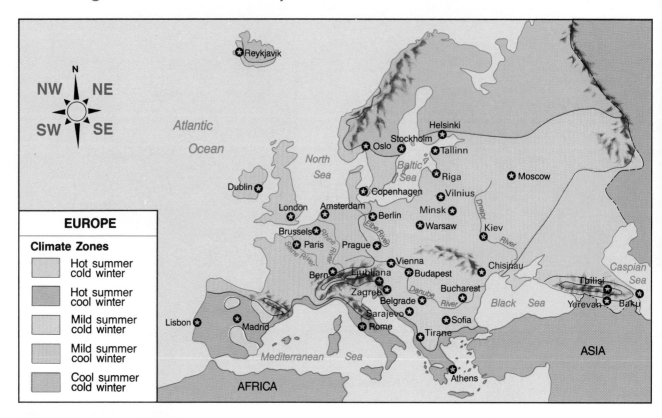

EUROPE

Climate Zones

- Hot summer cold winter
- Hot summer cool winter
- Mild summer cold winter
- Mild summer cool winter
- Cool summer cold winter

MAP ATTACK!

- **Read the title.** This map shows _____ Europe _____.
- **Read the compass rose.** Label the intermediate direction arrows.

1. What information is combined on this map?

   _____ relief and climate _____

2. Name one major water form near each of these climate zones.

   a. mild summer, cold winter _____ answers will vary _____

   b. hot summer, cold winter _____ answers will vary _____

   c. mild summer, cool winter _____ answers will vary _____

3. Name two cities in each of these climate zones.

   a. hot summer, cool winter _____ answers will vary _____

   b. mild summer, cool winter _____ answers will vary _____

   c. mild summer, cold winter _____ answers will vary _____

4. Find the Danube River. Name the capital cities that are along the

   Danube River. _____ Vienna, Budapest, Belgrade, Bucharest _____

Reading a Combined Map

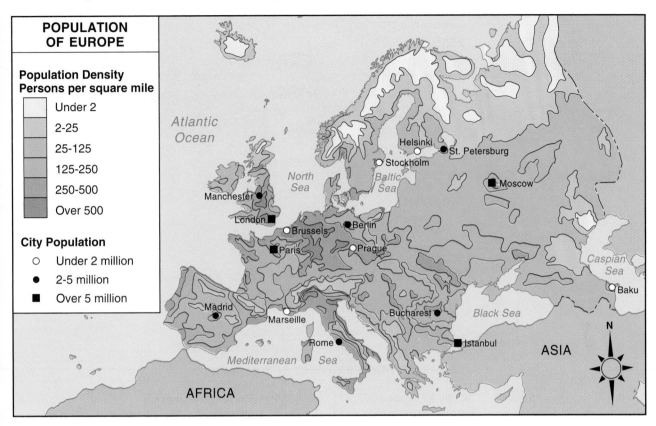

POPULATION OF EUROPE

**Population Density
Persons per square mile**

- Under 2
- 2-25
- 25-125
- 125-250
- 250-500
- Over 500

City Population

- ○ Under 2 million
- ● 2-5 million
- ■ Over 5 million

Atlantic Ocean

Helsinki ○ · St. Petersburg ●
○ Stockholm
Baltic Sea · ■ Moscow
North Sea
Manchester ●
London ■
○ Brussels · ■ Berlin
■ Paris · ○ Prague
Caspian Sea
○ Baku
Madrid ●
Marseille ○
Bucharest ● · Black Sea
Rome ● · ■ Istanbul
Mediterranean Sea
AFRICA
ASIA
N

1. Name four cities that have more than 5 million people.

   Moscow, London, Paris, and Istanbul

2. Name six cities that have 2 to 5 million people.

   St. Petersburg, Madrid, Berlin, Rome, Manchester, and Bucharest

3. Name six cities that have less than 2 million people.

   Stockholm, Helsinki, Marseille, Baku, Brussels, and Prague

4. Is the population density higher or lower around the cities? **higher**

   Why do you think this is so? **Answers will vary but could include that people tend to live close to the cities.**

5. What is the population density of most of the areas around the Baltic

   Sea? **25–125 persons per square mile**

6. Draw a conclusion. Look at the map on page 58. What climate zone has

   the lowest population density? **cool summer, cold winter**

   Why do you think this is so? **Answers will vary but could include that it is harder for people to live where it is very cold.**

Reading a Combined Map

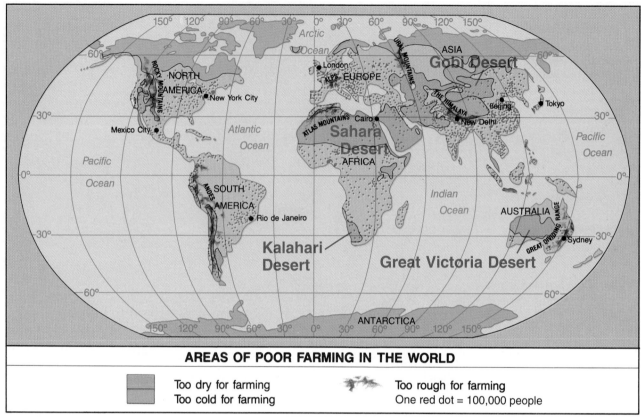

AREAS OF POOR FARMING IN THE WORLD

	Too dry for farming		Too rough for farming
	Too cold for farming		One red dot = 100,000 people

1. What two continents have the largest area of land too dry for farming?
   Africa and Asia

2. What continent is completely without a settled population?
   Antarctica

3. What continent is too cold for farming? **Antarctica**

4. What continent has the most areas of dense population? **Asia**

5. Label the following places on the map.
   Sahara Desert an area in northern Africa too dry for farming
   Gobi Desert an area north of the Himalaya too dry for farming
   Kalahari Desert an area in southern Africa too dry for farming
   Great Victoria Desert an area in western Australia too dry for farming

6. Draw a conclusion. Name three conditions that make land poor for farming. Then name one place in the world that fits each condition.

Condition	Place
too dry	**answers will vary**
too cold	**answers will vary**
too rough	**answers will vary**

Skill Check

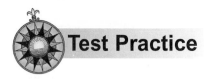

Vocabulary Check   **relationships**   **population density**

Write the word or phrase that best completes the sentence.

1. The number of people per square mile is _____population density_____.

2. You can find _____relationships_____ when you combine or compare facts.

Map Check

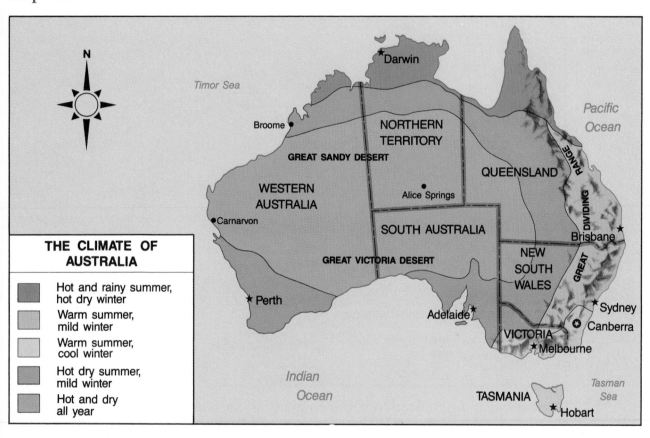

1. What is the climate of these cities?

   a. Sydney _____Warm summer, mild winter_____

   b. Darwin _____Hot and rainy summer, hot dry winter_____

   c. Alice Springs _____Hot and dry all year_____

   d. Perth _____Hot dry summer, mild winter_____

2. What is the climate of Tasmania? _____Warm summer, cool winter_____

3. How is the climate east of the Great Dividing Range different from

   the climate west of it? _____It is wetter and cooler to the east._____

4. Which state has the least variety in climate? _____Tasmania_____

Geography Themes Up Close

Human/Environment Interaction describes how people change or adapt to the environment. Some changes to the land cause problems. In North Africa, much of the land is desert. In what ways would a desert environment affect the people who live there? In some areas of North Africa, **desertification** has become a problem. Desertification is the spread of desert conditions into the neighboring environment. This results in an increase in the size of the desert.

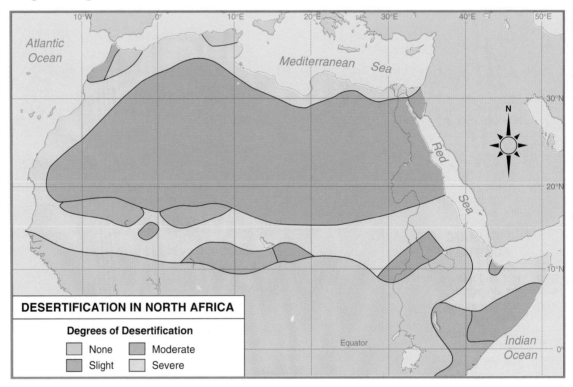

DESERTIFICATION IN NORTH AFRICA

Degrees of Desertification

None Moderate
Slight Severe

1. How much desertification is shown along the Mediterranean Sea?

   severe desertification

2. Describe the desertification between 10°N and 20°N latitudes.

   It is mostly severe desertification with moderate and slight

   desertification in some areas.

3. Explain why it would be helpful for geographers to know the locations, kinds, and causes of desertification in North Africa.

   Answers will vary, but students might state that it would be helpful to

   know which areas needed help, which areas should be helped first, and

   how to stop the desertification.

For hundreds of years, the Dutch people of the Netherlands have worked to **reclaim,** or take back, land that has been flooded. They built dikes around the flooded areas and drained the water. The Dutch call this reclaimed land "polders."

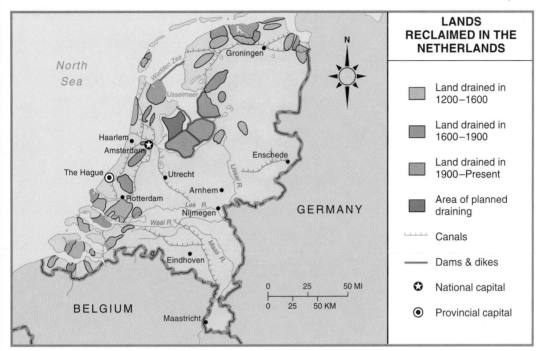

4. During which time period did the Dutch reclaim the most land?

   1900 to present

5. Along which bodies of water was land reclaimed?

   the North Sea and some rivers

6. What is the location of future polders?

   Near Amsterdam at IJsselmeer

7. Based on the map, how have the Dutch worked with their environment besides building polders, dams, and dikes?

   They have built canals.

8. How would you describe the interaction of the Dutch with their environment? How has it been beneficial or harmful? Explain.

   Answers will vary. Students might suggest that draining the water may cause some harmful effects on plants and wildlife that depended on that water, but overall, the interaction was beneficial to the people.

9 ⊕ Comparing Maps

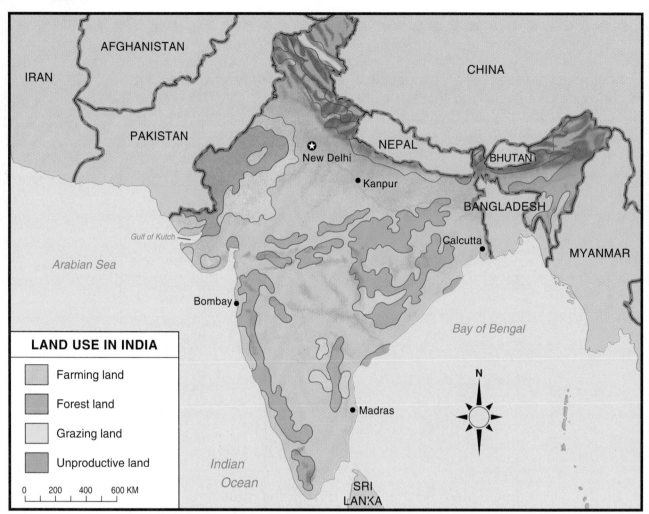

LAND USE IN INDIA

- ☐ Farming land
- ☐ Forest land
- ☐ Grazing land
- ☐ Unproductive land

0   200   400   600 KM

Comparing two maps of the same place can help you to get a better understanding of that place. The map on this page shows how land is used in India. The map on page 65 shows the products that are grown or mined in each region of India. Before you begin comparing the maps, use your **Map Attack!** skills to become familiar with each map.

- ● **Read the title.** What can you expect to learn from each map?
- ● **Read the legend.** Find an example of each land use on this map. Find an example of each resource on the next map.
- ● **Read the compass rose.** Find north on each map.
- ● **Read the scale.** Are distances measured in miles or kilometers? Is the scale the same on both maps?

After you are familiar with each map, study each map separately to see what you can learn. Read the facts on each map.

► India's unproductive land is mostly in which region? **north and northwest**

► India's northeast region is mostly used for what? **farming and forest**

► What is the most widespread land use in India? **farming**

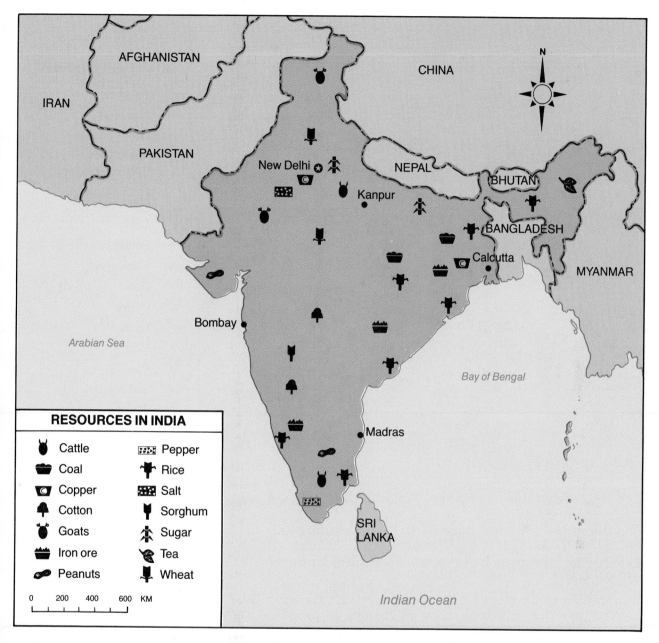

RESOURCES IN INDIA

Cattle		Pepper	
Coal		Rice	
Copper		Salt	
Cotton		Sorghum	
Goats		Sugar	
Iron ore		Tea	
Peanuts		Wheat	

0   200   400   600   KM

Once you are familiar with each map, you can begin comparing them. To compare land use and resources in the southern tip of India, first find the southern tip of India on each map. Make sure you are looking at the same area of India on each map. Is the pepper from southern India found in forest or farm land? **forest**

Now compare other areas of India. Use the legend of each map to help you answer these questions.

► What is the land use in most coal-mining areas of India? **forest**

► What is the land use in the area where goats are a product? **grazing land**

► What is the land use where salt is mined? **grazing land**

► What is the land use around each of these manufacturing centers?

       Calcutta   Bombay   Madras   New Delhi
       farming   **farming**   **farming**   **farming**

► What resources are found near those manufacturing centers? **Calcutta: copper; Bombay: no resources; Madras: no resources; New Delhi: sugar, copper**

Comparing Maps

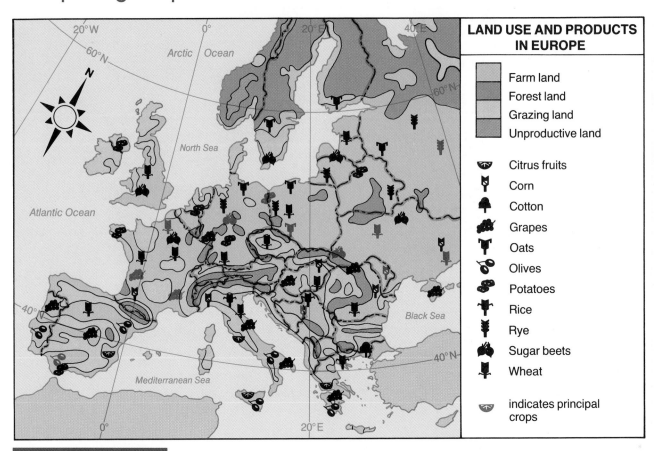

LAND USE AND PRODUCTS IN EUROPE

- Farm land
- Forest land
- Grazing land
- Unproductive land

- Citrus fruits
- Corn
- Cotton
- Grapes
- Oats
- Olives
- Potatoes
- Rice
- Rye
- Sugar beets
- Wheat

indicates principal crops

MAP ATTACK!

Follow the steps on page 64 to begin reading this map.

1. What are the principal crops in southern Europe?

   olives, grapes, corn

2. What are the principal crops in eastern Europe?

   sugar beets, wheat, corn, rye

3. What is the main land use in Europe north of 60°N?

   It is forest.

4. Where are Europe's largest forests? _____ **in the north** _____
5. What is the main land use north of the Black Sea?

   It is farm land.

6. Circle the crops most often grown where grapes are grown.

   rye   cotton   oats   (olives)   (citrus fruits)   corn   (wheat)

7. Circle the crops most often grown where wheat is grown.

   (sugar beets)   (rye)   (oats)   cotton   (potatoes)   olives   (grapes)

Comparing Maps

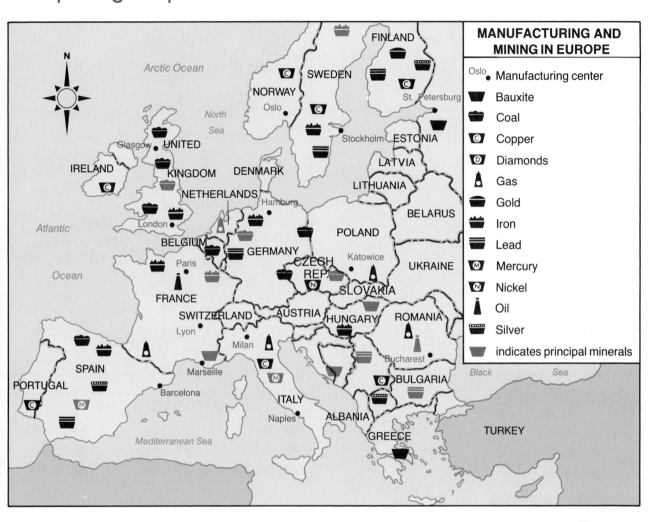

MANUFACTURING AND MINING IN EUROPE

- Oslo● Manufacturing center
- Bauxite
- Coal
- Copper
- Diamonds
- Gas
- Gold
- Iron
- Lead
- Mercury
- Nickel
- Oil
- Silver
- indicates principal minerals

1. Name five manufacturing centers in southern Europe.

   Barcelona, Marseille, Lyon, Milan, Naples, Bucharest

2. Name five manufacturing centers in northern Europe.

   Glasgow, London, Paris, Hamburg, Oslo, Stockholm, Katowice, or St. Petersburg

3. Circle the principal crops and minerals in each of these countries.

   a. France   (bauxite)   (grapes)   gold   (wheat)   (iron)

   b. Spain   oats   (olives)   (mercury)   grapes   gas

   c. Italy   copper   rice   oil   corn   (mercury)

4. List the mining and farming industries in each of these countries.

   a. Greece   **cotton, rice, citrus fruits, grapes, olives, bauxite**

   b. Italy   **corn, rice, wheat, grapes, citrus fruits, olives, gas, copper, mercury**

   c. Hungary   **corn, wheat, grapes, bauxite, iron**

Comparing Maps

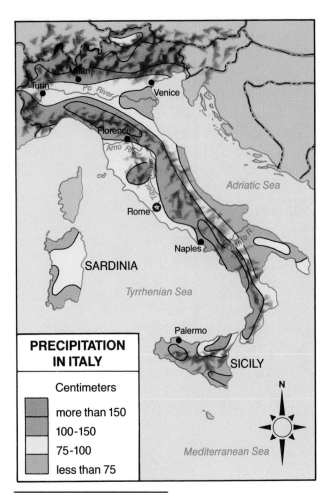

PRECIPITATION IN ITALY

Centimeters

	more than 150
	100-150
	75-100
	less than 75

RESOURCES IN ITALY

	Coal		Hogs		Poultry
	Goats		Lumber		Sheep
	Grapes		Olives		Sulfur

MAP ATTACK!

Follow the steps on page 64 to compare the maps.

1. Circle the resources that are found near each city.

   a. Rome   (olives)   lumber   (hogs)   (sheep)   coal

   b. Florence   goats   olives   (sheep)   (grapes)   hogs

   c. Turin   sheep   (coal)   (grapes)   poultry   olives

2. Name three resources found along the Po River.

   grapes, hogs, sulfur, coal

3. Name three resources found mostly in the northern mountains.

   sheep, sulfur, goats, coal, poultry

4. Name two resources found mostly in drier areas. **grapes, sheet**

5. Name three resources found in the rainy area of northern Italy.

   Answers should include three of the following:
   lumber, goats, sheep, coal, poultry, hogs, sulfur.

Skill Check

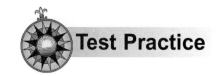
Vocabulary Check   **comparing**

Circle the best ending for the following sentence.

Comparing two different maps of the same place is

   a. necessary for you to determine directions.

   (b.) a good way to help you understand the place.

   c. the only way to learn about a country's products.

Map Check

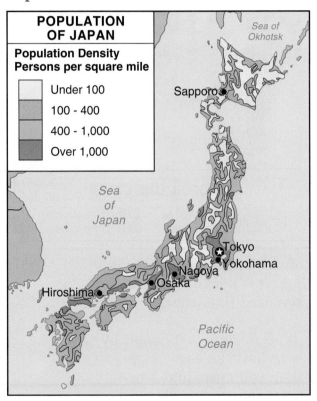

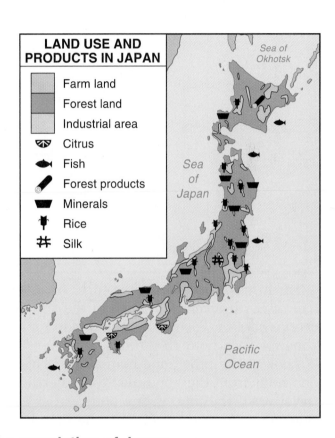

1. a. The map on the left shows _____the population of Japan_____.

   b. The map on the right shows _____land use and products in Japan_____.

2. Is the population density of Japan higher along the coasts or inland?

   _____along the coasts_____

3. What is Japan's chief crop? _____rice_____

4. Does Japan have more farm land or forest land? _____forest land_____

5. Is the population density of Japan higher in the farming areas or the

   industrial areas? _____in the industrial areas_____

6. What products are found near Sapporo? _____minerals, rice_____

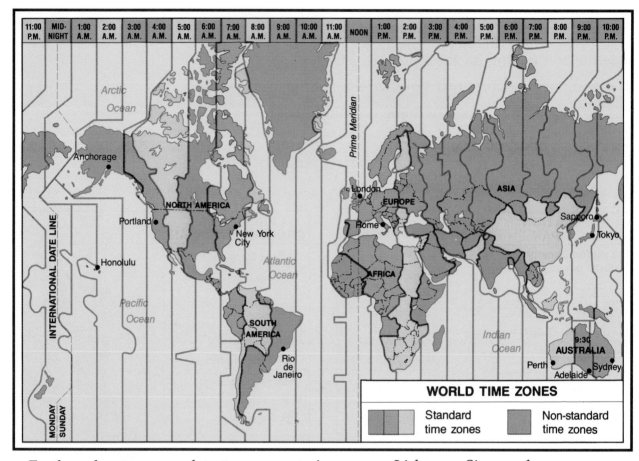

| 11:00 P.M. | MID-NIGHT | 1:00 A.M. | 2:00 A.M. | 3:00 A.M. | 4:00 A.M. | 5:00 A.M. | 6:00 A.M. | 7:00 A.M. | 8:00 A.M. | 9:00 A.M. | 10:00 A.M. | 11:00 A.M. | NOON | 1:00 P.M. | 2:00 P.M. | 3:00 P.M. | 4:00 P.M. | 5:00 P.M. | 6:00 P.M. | 7:00 P.M. | 8:00 P.M. | 9:00 P.M. | 10:00 P.M. |

WORLD TIME ZONES

Standard time zones   Non-standard time zones

Earth makes one complete turn, or rotation, every 24 hours. Since only half of Earth receives light from the sun at a time, it is not the same time everywhere on Earth. Earth is divided into 24 **standard time zones**, one time zone for each hour in the day.

Look at the time zone map above. The time in each zone is different by one hour from the zone next to it. Earth rotates toward the east. So as you travel west, the time is one hour earlier every time you cross into a new time zone. As you travel east, the time is one hour later.

Find London on the Prime Meridian (0 degrees). It is in the time zone labeled NOON. Now find Rome. It is one time zone east of London, so the time is one hour later. When it is 12:00 noon in London, it is 1:00 P.M. in Rome. Now find Rio de Janeiro. It is three time zones west of London, so the time is three hours earlier. When it is 12:00 noon in London, it is 9:00 A.M. in Rio de Janeiro.

Find New York City. How many time zones is it from London? Which direction is it from London? What time is it in New York City when it is 12:00 noon in London? It is 7 A.M. in New York City.

Notice that the time zones often follow political boundaries. This keeps places in one state, country, or area all in the same time zone. Some places around the world do not observe standard time zones and use different times. Find central Australia on the map. Notice that in Adelaide it is 9:30 when it is 8:00 in Perth.

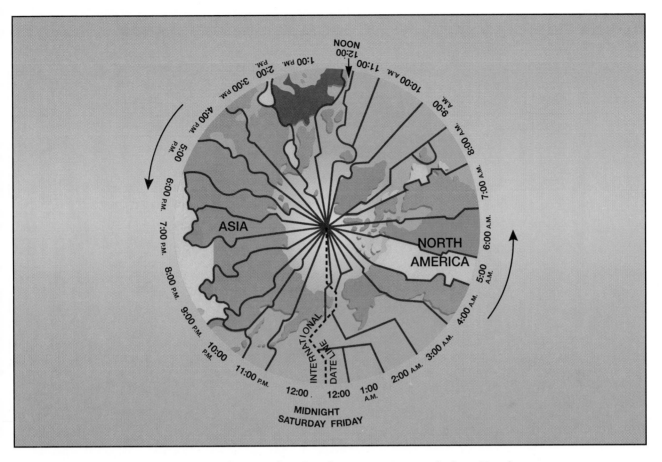

Remember that it takes 24 hours for Earth to rotate, and that Earth rotates toward the east. If you traveled west around Earth for 24 hours, you would set your watch back every time you entered a new time zone. When you arrived at home, your watch would show the same hour as when you left. But it would actually be 24 hours later—the next day.

Find the **International Date Line** on the drawing above. This imaginary line, at about 180° longitude, separates one day from the next. The time of day is the same on both sides of the line. But west of the line it is one day later than it is to the east. If it is midnight Sunday on the east side of the line, it is midnight Monday on the west side of the line.

Notice that the International Date Line does not follow the 180° line of longitude exactly. It goes around various countries to keep places in one political area in the same time zone and day.

Find Portland, Oregon, on the map on page 70. Suppose you start traveling west from Portland at 4:00 A.M. Friday morning. It is midnight at the Date Line. On the east side it is midnight Friday. But on the west side it is midnight Saturday. After you cross the Date Line, you enter late Saturday night. You actually miss one day, almost all of Friday. Farther west of the Date Line it is late evening on Saturday. In Sapporo it is 9:00 P.M. Saturday.

► Asia is west of the International Date Line. North America is east of the International Date Line. Look at the drawing above. If it is Monday in Asia, what day is it in North America? **Sunday**

► Look at the map on page 70. If it is 3:00 P.M. on Tuesday in Anchorage, Alaska, what is the day and time in Sydney, Australia? **10 A.M. Wednesday**

Reading a Time Zone Map

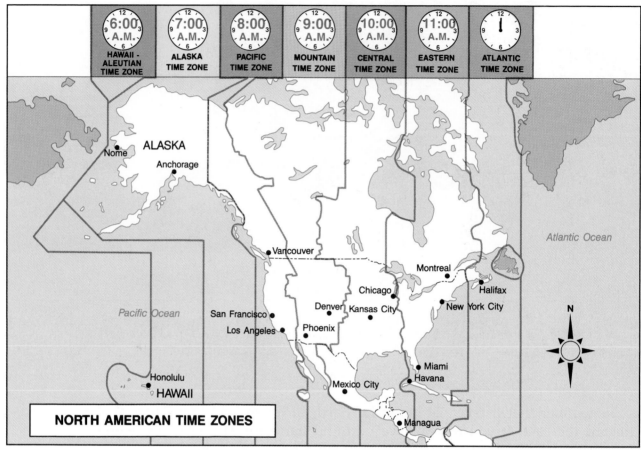

NORTH AMERICAN TIME ZONES

Time zones colored to match directions.

1. Lightly color the time zones. Match the colors at the top of the map. Follow the lines along state boundaries or physical features.

2. It is 12:00 noon in the Atlantic Time Zone. Write the correct times on the clocks for the other time zones. Remember, the time is one hour earlier as you travel west.

3. If it is 8:00 A.M. in Los Angeles, what time is it in each city listed below?

a. Vancouver __8:00 A.M.__

e. Miami __11:00 A.M.__

b. Kansas City __10:00 A.M.__

f. Denver __9:00 A.M.__

c. Honolulu __6:00 A.M.__

g. New York City __11:00 A.M.__

d. Anchorage __7:00 A.M.__

h. Halifax __12:00 NOON__

4. The World Series is at 6:00 P.M. in New York City. What time is it in each city listed below?

a. Montreal __6:00 P.M.__

d. Phoenix __4:00 P.M.__

b. Mexico City __5:00 P.M.__

e. San Francisco __3:00 P.M.__

c. Nome __2:00 P.M.__

f. Honolulu __1:00 P.M.__

Mastering World Time Zones

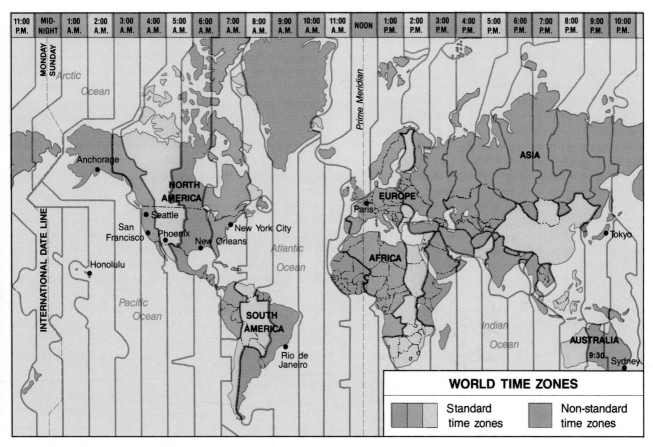

| 11:00 P.M. | MID-NIGHT | 1:00 A.M. | 2:00 A.M. | 3:00 A.M. | 4:00 A.M. | 5:00 A.M. | 6:00 A.M. | 7:00 A.M. | 8:00 A.M. | 9:00 A.M. | 10:00 A.M. | 11:00 A.M. | NOON | 1:00 P.M. | 2:00 P.M. | 3:00 P.M. | 4:00 P.M. | 5:00 P.M. | 6:00 P.M. | 7:00 P.M. | 8:00 P.M. | 9:00 P.M. | 10:00 P.M. |

WORLD TIME ZONES

Standard time zones   Non-standard time zones

1. Which continents have a large area without standard time? Look at the colors in the map key.

   _____Asia, Australia, and Europe_____

2. How many time zones does each of these continents have?

   a. Africa _____four_____   b. South America _____three_____

3. If you go from Tokyo to Sydney, how many time zones do you cross?

   _____one_____

4. If you go from Seattle to Rio de Janeiro, how many time zones do

   you cross? _____four or five, depending on the route taken_____

5. If you go from Honolulu to New Orleans, how many time zones do

   you cross? _____four_____

6. It is 7:00 A.M. in Phoenix. What time is it in Paris? _____3:00 P.M._____

7. It is 3:00 P.M. in Rio de Janeiro. What time is it in San Francisco?

   _____10:00 A.M._____

8. Suppose you fly from Anchorage to New York City. Do you move

   your watch ahead or back? _____ahead_____ How many hours? _____four_____

Mastering World Time Zones

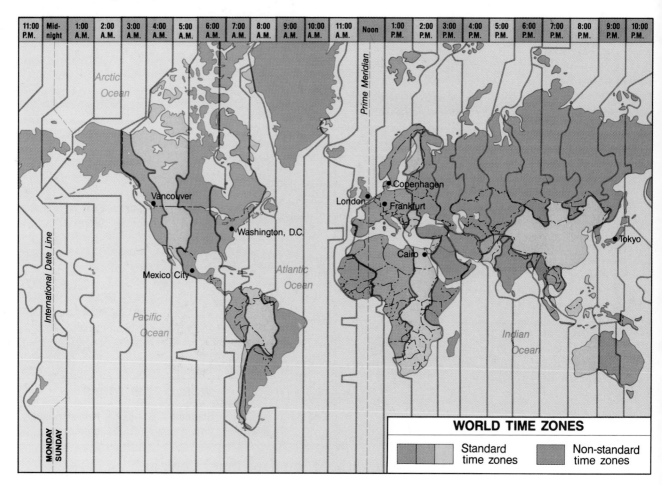

| 11:00 P.M. | Mid-night | 1:00 A.M. | 2:00 A.M. | 3:00 A.M. | 4:00 A.M. | 5:00 A.M. | 6:00 A.M. | 7:00 A.M. | 8:00 A.M. | 9:00 A.M. | 10:00 A.M. | 11:00 A.M. | Noon | 1:00 P.M. | 2:00 P.M. | 3:00 P.M. | 4:00 P.M. | 5:00 P.M. | 6:00 P.M. | 7:00 P.M. | 8:00 P.M. | 9:00 P.M. | 10:00 P.M. |

WORLD TIME ZONES

Standard time zones   Non-standard time zones

1. You are planning trips from London to various places around the world. Finish the chart below. Write the direction from London to each city. Then write whether you set your watch ahead (+) or back (−), and by how many hours. The first one is done for you.

From London to	Direction	Set Watch	How Many Hours
a. Frankfurt	east	+	1
b. Cairo	southeast	+	2
c. Tokyo	southeast	+	9
d. Mexico City	southwest	−	6
e. Washington, D.C.	southwest	−	5
f. Copenhagen	northeast	+	1
g. Vancouver	west	−	8

2. If it is 12:01 P.M. Tuesday in Frankfurt, what time and day is it halfway around the world? **12:01 A.M. Tuesday**

Skill Check

Vocabulary Check   standard time zones   International Date Line

Write the words that best complete each sentence.

1. Earth has 24 _____ standard time zones _____.

2. When you go west across the _____ International Date Line _____
it is suddenly tomorrow, and you lose a day.

Map Check

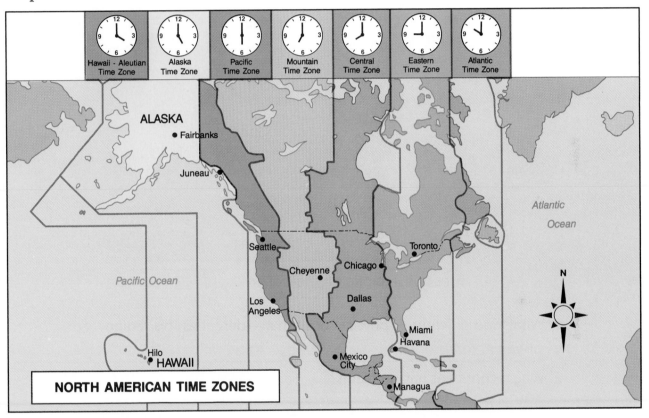

NORTH AMERICAN TIME ZONES

1. Dallas is in the _____ Central _____ Time Zone.

2. Seattle is in the _____ Pacific _____ Time Zone.

3. Toronto is in the _____ Eastern _____ Time Zone.

4. Fairbanks is in the _____ Alaska _____ Time Zone.

5. The President gave a speech at 9:00 P.M. Eastern Time. What time was it
in these cities?

    a. Los Angeles _____ 6:00 P.M. _____   d. Havana _____ 9:00 P.M. _____

    b. Chicago _____ 8:00 P.M. _____   e. Cheyenne _____ 7:00 P.M. _____

    c. Hilo _____ 4:00 P.M. _____   f. Juneau _____ 5:00 P.M. _____

Geography Themes Up Close

Regions are places that are similar in one or more ways. Geographers categorize areas into regions based on one feature, such as the climate or type of government. They also recognize regions by a number of features, such as landforms, soil, language, history, and culture.

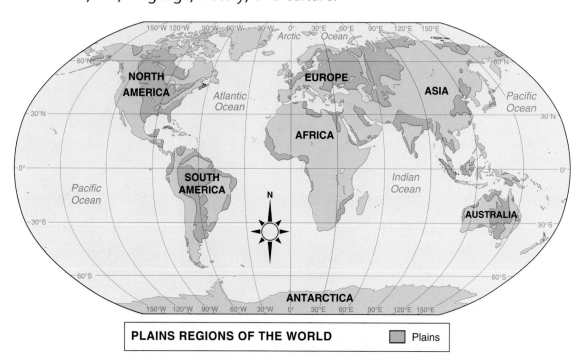

PLAINS REGIONS OF THE WORLD ⬛ Plains

1. What kind of feature—physical or human—describes this region?

   physical feature

2. Which continent has no plains?

   Antarctica

3. In what part of South America are plains mostly located?

   in central South America

4. In what two ways might plains regions differ from mountain regions of the world?

   Answers will vary, but students might suggest that since plains are

   flatter than mountains, they are more easily settled and farmed than

   are mountains, therefore having larger populations. There might also

   be differences in climate or temperature.

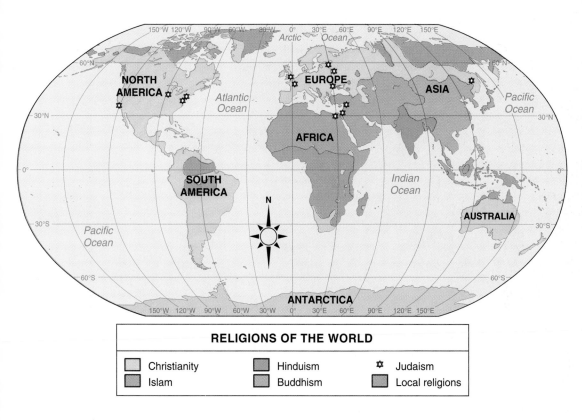

RELIGIONS OF THE WORLD

☐ Christianity	☐ Hinduism	✡ Judaism
☐ Islam	☐ Buddhism	☐ Local religions

5. What kind of feature—physical or human—describes the regions on this map?

human feature

6. In what parts of the world is Islam a major religion?

Middle East, North Africa, Bangladesh, Pakistan, central Asia, and

Southeast Asia

7. What is the major religion of North America?

Christianity

8. In what parts of the world is Judaism practiced?

Europe, the Middle East, United States, and eastern Russia

9. Why might knowing the major religion of a region help you understand more about the region?

Answers will vary, but students might point out that ways of life in

regions are influenced by the religion practiced there.

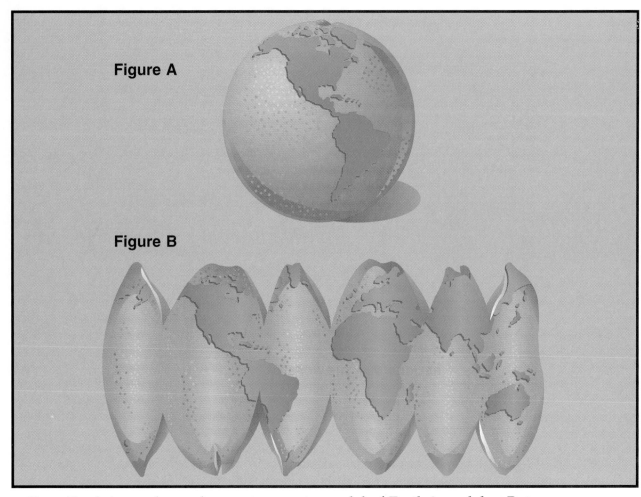

Figure A

Figure B

Since Earth is a sphere, the most accurate model of Earth is a globe. But often it is more useful to have a flat map of Earth. **Cartographers**—people who make maps—have made many flat maps of Earth.

Making a flat map of spherical Earth is not an easy task. To understand why, look at Figure A, which shows an orange made into a globe. Now imagine peeling the curved surface off the orange and making it lie flat. To do this, you need to stretch and tear the orange peel. Figure B shows the results. This action—taking a curved surface and forcing it to lie flat—is exactly what cartographers have to do when they make a flat map of the curved surface of Earth.

Look at the illustrations again. Notice how the shapes of the continents were changed when the curved peel was stretched flat. This change in a curved surface when it is flattened is called **distortion**. Every map of Earth has distortion. To draw a flat map of spherical Earth, parts of the sphere must be distorted, just as the orange peel must be distorted to make it lie flat.

Different maps distort Earth in different ways. Some maps distort the shape of continents. Other maps distort the size. The type of distortion a map has depends on its projection. A **projection** is the way in which a cartographer projects, or shows, the curved surface of Earth on a flat map. A cartographer chooses the type of projection to use based on the purpose of the map.

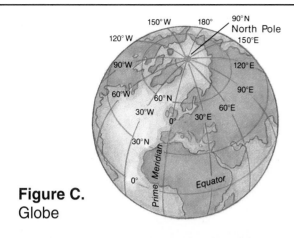

Figure C.
Globe

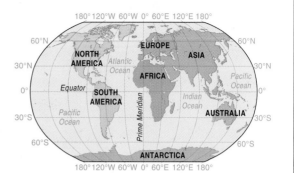

Figure E. Robinson Projection

Figure D. Mercator Projection

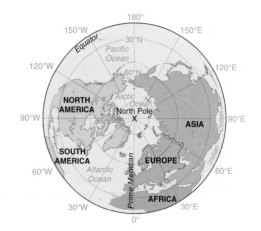

Figure F. North Polar Projection

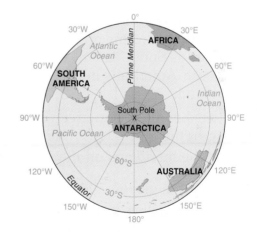

Figure G. South Polar Projection

There are many different kinds of map projections. A few of the most common ones are pictured here.

Look first at the drawing of the globe in Figure C. It shows the grid lines of latitude and longitude. As you look at each map projection, compare the grid on it with the grid on the drawing of the globe. This will help you see how each projection distorts the surface of Earth.

The map in Figure D is a **Mercator projection**. It is named after Gerhardus Mercator, a Flemish cartographer who lived in the 1500s. The Mercator projection is one of the most common map projections.

The map in Figure E is a **Robinson projection**. It is named after the American cartographer Arthur Robinson. This projection is becoming more popular.

The maps in Figures F and G are **polar projections**. Why do you think these projections are called polar projections? **They are centered on the poles.**

▶ Turn to the world map on page 74. What type of projection is it? **Mercator**

▶ Turn to the world map on page 60. What type of projection is it? **Robinson**

Reading a Mercator Projection

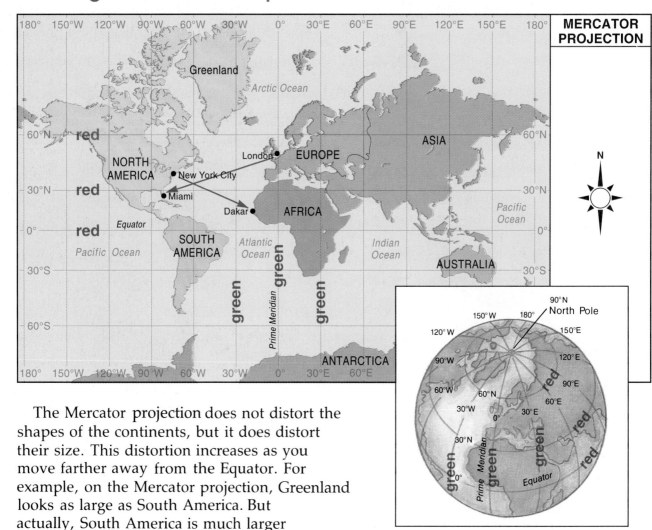

The Mercator projection does not distort the shapes of the continents, but it does distort their size. This distortion increases as you move farther away from the Equator. For example, on the Mercator projection, Greenland looks as large as South America. But actually, South America is much larger than Greenland.

1. Trace these meridians in green on both the Mercator projection and the drawing of the globe: 0° (Prime Meridian), 30°E, 30°W.

   How do the meridians on the Mercator projection differ from those on the drawing of the globe? __Mercator meridians are straight and do not meet.__

2. Trace these parallels in red on both the Mercator projection and the drawing of the globe: 0° (Equator), 30°N, 60°N.

   How do the parallels on the Mercator projection differ from those on the drawing of the globe? __Mercator parallels are straight and do not curve.__

3. An important advantage of the Mercator projection is that it does not distort directions. It is often used by sailors, who rely on accurate compass directions for navigation. Draw an arrow on the map from the first place to the second place. Write the direction of travel.

   a. London to Miami _____SW_____

   b. New York City to Dakar _____SE_____

Reading a Robinson Projection

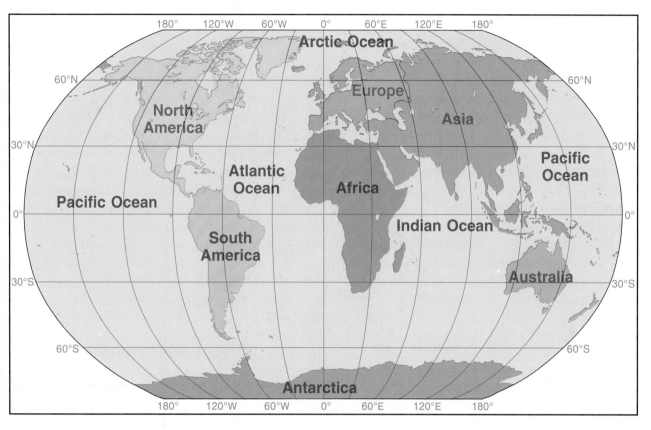

Every flat map of Earth has distortion. The Robinson projection is no different. It shows Antarctica as much larger than it actually is. Yet to many people, the Robinson projection looks more like a globe than most other projections. This is because the Robinson projection is a compromise of many map distortions. You can think of a Robinson projection as having many small distortions instead of a few large ones. The result is a map that looks very much like a globe.

1. Label the seven continents on the Robinson projection above: North America, South America, Europe, Africa, Asia, Australia, and Antarctica.

2. Label these four oceans on the map: Arctic Ocean, Pacific Ocean, Atlantic Ocean, and Indian Ocean. (Label both areas of the Pacific Ocean.)

3. a. Are the parallels on the Robinson projection curved or straight? __straight__
   b. How do these compare with the parallels on a Mercator projection?

   __They are the same.__

4. a. Are the meridians on a Robinson projection curved or straight? __curved__
   b. How do these compare with the meridians on a Mercator projection?
   __Mercator meridians are straight.__

5. Draw a conclusion. Why do you think the Robinson projection shows a small part of Asia on the left-hand side of the map, when most of Asia is shown on the right-hand side? __to show that Earth is a sphere__

Reading Polar Projections

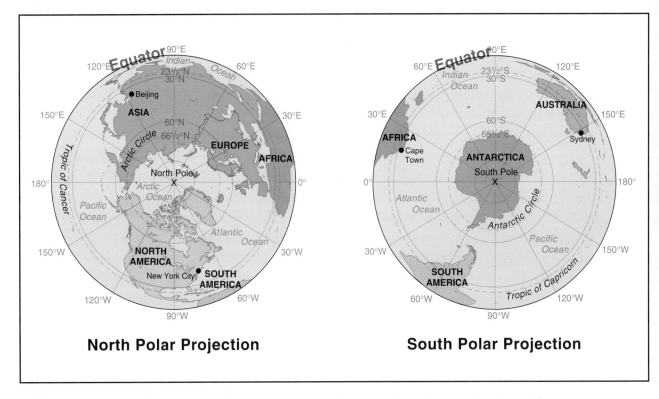

North Polar Projection

South Polar Projection

The two maps above are polar projections. In a north polar projection, the North Pole is at the center of the map. In a south polar projection, the South Pole is at the center. Polar projections usually show one hemisphere. Like all flat maps of Earth, polar projections have distortion. Polar projections are more distorted toward the edges.

1. a. Which hemisphere is shown on a north polar projection? __Northern__

   b. Which hemisphere is shown on a south polar projection? __Southern__

2. Label the Equator on each of the two maps above.

3. Usually, north is at the top of a map. In a north polar projection, however, this isn't the case. Remember, the direction north is the direction toward the North Pole. In a north polar projection, the North Pole is in the center of the map. If you go from any point on the map toward the center, you are going north. Imagine you are traveling from the first place to the second place. Which direction will you travel?

   a. New York City to the North Pole _____north_____

   b. the North Pole to Beijing _____south_____

4. The direction south is the direction toward the South Pole. Study the south polar projection above. Imagine you are traveling from the first place to the second place. Which direction will you travel?

   a. Cape Town to the South Pole _____south_____

   b. the South Pole to Sydney _____north_____

Skill Check

Vocabulary Check

Mercator projection
Robinson projection
distortion

cartographers
polar projection
projection

Write the term that best completes each sentence.

1. People who make maps are known as _____ cartographers _____ .

2. Because all projections of Earth show a curved surface on a flat map, they
have _____ distortion _____ .

3. The _____ Mercator projection _____ was created for sailors in the 1500s.

Map Check

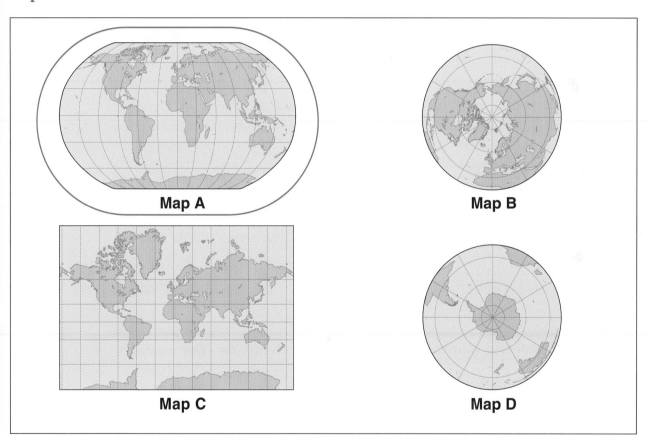

Map A

Map B

Map C

Map D

1. Identify each map projection.

   a. Map A is a _____ Robinson _____ projection.

   b. Map B is a _____ north polar _____ projection.

   c. Map C is a _____ Mercator _____ projection.

   d. Map D is a _____ south polar _____ projection.

2. Circle the projection that most closely resembles a globe.

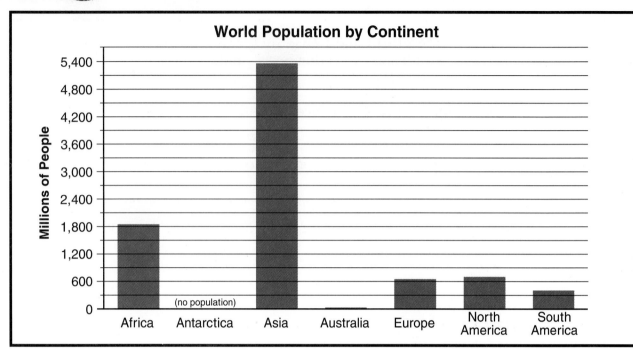

Information can be presented in graphs to make it easy to read. Bars on a **bar graph** stand for amounts. The bars make it easy to compare the amounts at a glance.

GRAPH ATTACK!

Follow these steps to read and use the bar graph.

1. Read the title. This bar graph shows __world population by continent__ .

2. Read the labels at the bottom of the graph. Name the areas shown on the graph. __Africa, Antarctica, Asia, Australia, Europe, North America, and South America__

3. Read the label and numbers on the left side of the graph. The numbers on the graph stand for __millions of people__ .

4. Compare the bars.

   a. The continent with the largest population is __Asia__ .

   b. The continent with no population is __Antarctica__ .

   c. Estimate the population of North America. __720 million__

   d. List the continents in order from greatest to least population. __Asia, Africa, North America, Europe, South America, Australia, Antarctica__

5. Draw a conclusion. The population of Europe is between the population of what two other continents? __North America and South America__

Reading a Bar Graph

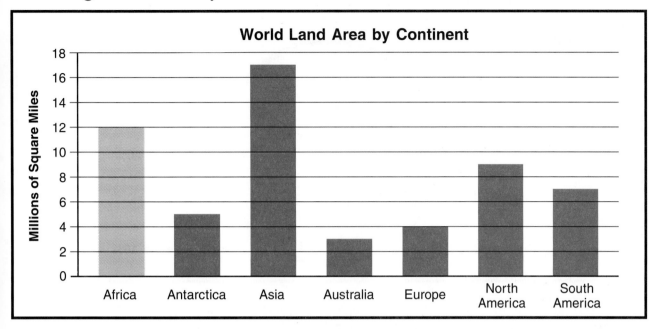

World Land Area by Continent

1. **Read the title.** This bar graph shows _world land area by continent_.
2. **Read the labels at the bottom of the graph.** Name the areas shown on the graph. _Africa, Antarctica, Asia, Australia, Europe, North America,_
   and South America
3. **Read the label and numbers on the left side of the graph.** The numbers on the graph stand for _millions of square miles_.
4. **Finish the graph.** Add bars to the graph to show the approximate area in square miles of the following continents:

Antarctica	5 million	Europe	4 million
Asia	17 million	North America	9 million
Australia	3 million	South America	7 million

5. **Compare the bars.**

   a. The largest continent is _Asia_.

   b. The smallest continent is _Australia_.

   c. Estimate the area of Africa. _12 million square miles_

6. **Compare graphs and draw a conclusion.**

   a. How do Africa and Europe compare in land area? _Africa is much larger._

   b. Look back at the bar graph for population on page 84. How do Africa and Europe compare in population? _Europe's population is slightly larger._

   c. Based on this information, do you think that Africa or Europe has more people per square mile? _Europe has more people per square mile._

Circle Graphs

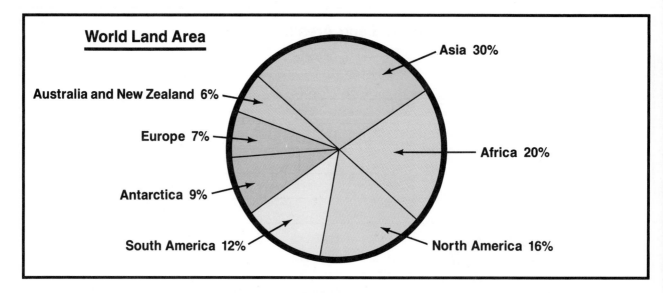

World Land Area

Australia and New Zealand 6%

Europe 7%

Antarctica 9%

South America 12%

Asia 30%

Africa 20%

North America 16%

A **circle graph** shows the parts that make up a whole set of facts. Each part of the graph is a percentage of the whole. All the parts together equal 100%. The circle graph on this page shows what percentage of all the land on Earth each continent includes.

GRAPH ATTACK!

Follow these steps to read the circle graph.

1. Read the title. The whole circle stands for _____world land area_____.
2. Read each part of the circle.

   a. Which continents are shown in this graph? _____Asia, Africa, North_____ _____America, South America, Antarctica, Europe, Australia_____.

   b. What percentage of Earth does each continent cover?

   North America __16%__   Europe __7%__   Asia __30%__

   South America __12%__   Africa __20%__   Antarctica __9%__

   c. Which continent covers the largest area of Earth's surface? __Asia__

   d. Which continent covers the smallest area? __Australia__

3. Compare the parts. Write <u>larger</u> or <u>smaller</u>.

   a. Asia is _____larger_____ than Africa.

   b. Europe is ___larger___ than Australia and New Zealand.

   c. Australia and New Zealand are ___smaller___ than North America.

4. Draw a conclusion. Europe and Antarctica together are the same size as what continent? __North America__

Comparing Graphs

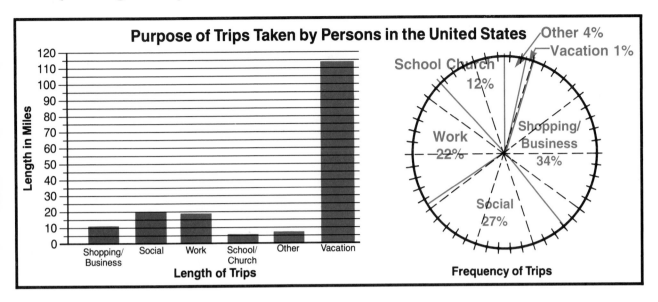

Purpose of Trips Taken by Persons in the United States

Length of Trips — bar graph: Length in Miles (y-axis 0 to 120) for Shopping/Business, Social, Work, School/Church, Other, Vacation

Frequency of Trips — circle graph: School Church 12%, Other 4%, Vacation 1%, Work 22%, Shopping/Business 34%, Social 27%

1. Read the title.

   a. The bars on the bar graph and the parts of the circle graph stand

   for _____the purpose of trips taken by persons in the U.S._____.

   b. The bar graph shows _____length of trips in miles_____.

   c. The circle graph will show _____frequency of trips_____.

2. Finish the circle graph. Each dotted section represents 10% of the circle. Use the information below to finish the graph. Color and label each part.

   Shopping/Business 34%   Social 27%   Work   22%
   School/Church   12%   Other 4%   Vacation 1%

3. Read each graph.

   a. The longest trip is for _____vacation_____.

   b. The shortest trip is for _____school/church_____.

   c. Most trips are for _____shopping/business_____.

   d. The fewest number of trips are for _____vacation_____.

4. Compare the graphs.

   a. Which trip is the longest and taken least often? _____vacation_____

   b. What is the length of the trip which is most often taken? _11 to 12 miles_

   c. Not including vacation, what two trips are longest?

   _____social and work_____

   d. Out of 100 trips taken, how many are long trips? _____49_____

Line Graphs

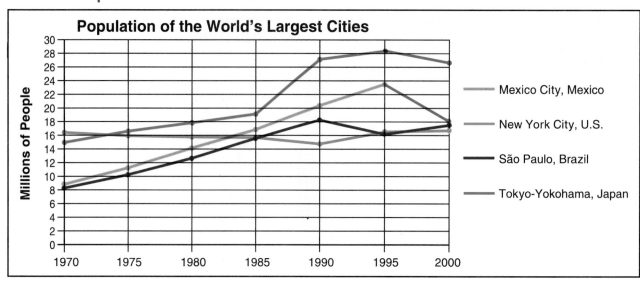

Population of the World's Largest Cities

(Y-axis: Millions of People — 0, 2, 4, 6, 8, 10, 12, 14, 16, 18, 20, 22, 24, 26, 28, 30)
(X-axis: 1970, 1975, 1980, 1985, 1990, 1995, 2000)

Key:
- Mexico City, Mexico
- New York City, U.S.
- São Paulo, Brazil
- Tokyo-Yokohama, Japan

A **line graph** shows how amounts increase, decrease, or stay the same over periods of time. These general directions are called trends.

GRAPH ATTACK!

Follow these steps to read and use the line graph.

1. Read the title. This line graph shows **population of the world's largest cities**.
2. Read the numbers at the bottom of the graph. What do these numbers indicate? **years**
3. Read the label and numbers on the left side of the graph. The numbers on the graph stand for **millions of people**.
4. Read the graph key. What does each line on the graph stand for? **the population of a city**
5. Finish the graph. Use the information below to complete the graph.
   Population of Tokyo-Yokohama in 2000 = 26.4 million
   Population of Mexico City in 2000 = 18 million
6. Compare the lines.
   a. Which city had the largest population in 1970? **New York City**
   b. Which city had the largest population in 1990? **Tokyo-Yokohama**
   c. In what years did São Paulo and New York City have about the same population? **1985 and 1995**
7. Draw a conclusion. The trend of the population of Mexico City is upwards. What is the trend of the population of New York City between 1970 and 1990? **slightly downwards**

Combining Line and Bar Graphs

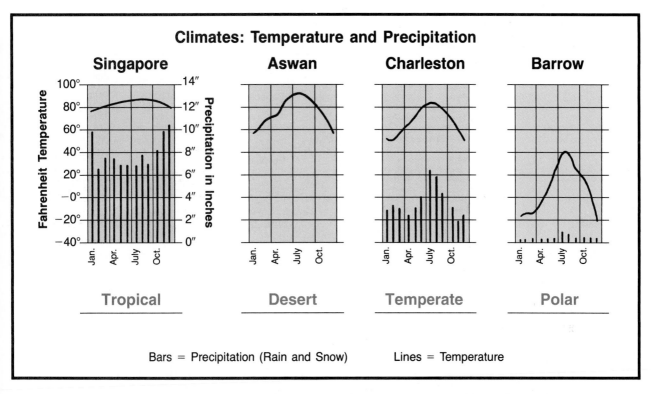

Climates: Temperature and Precipitation

Singapore

Fahrenheit Temperature

Precipitation in Inches

Tropical

Aswan

Desert

Charleston

Temperate

Barrow

Polar

Bars = Precipitation (Rain and Snow)   Lines = Temperature

1. Read the title. The graphs show __Climates: Temperature and Precipitation__.
2. Read the numbers along the sides of the graph. The numbers on the

   left sides indicate ___degrees of Fahrenheit temperature___.

   The numbers on the right sides indicate ___precipitation in inches___.

3. Read the words along the bottom. The words indicate ___bars and lines___.
4. Compare the graphs.
   a. Which place has the greatest amount of precipitation?

      ___Singapore___

   b. Which place has the lowest temperature? ___Barrow___
   c. Which place has the least change in temperature over the year?

      ___Singapore___

   d. Which place has the greatest change in precipitation over the year?

      ___Charleston___

5. Draw a conclusion. Label each place with the climate zone that best
   fits it.

   Temperate = warm and rainy summer, mild and rainy winter
   Desert = hot and dry all year
   Tropical = hot and rainy all year
   Polar = cold and dry all year

Tables

Eight Countries of the World

Country	Area (in sq. kilometers)	Capital	Official Language	Unit of Currency	Population	Highest Point (in meters)
Brazil	8,511,957	Brasília	Portuguese	Real	162,661,000	3014 Pico da Neblina
Canada	9,976,186	Ottawa	French; English	Canadian dollar	28,821,000	6050 Mt. Logan
Denmark	43,075	Copenhagen	Danish	Krone	5,250,000	173 Yding Skovhoj
Egypt	1,002,000	Cairo	Arabic	Egyptian pound	63,575,000	2637 Jabai Katrinah
Italy	301,278	Rome	Italian	Lira	57,460,000	4731 Mt. Blanc
New Zealand	270,534	Wallington	English	New Zealand dollar	3,548,000	3764 Mt. Cook
Tanzania	945,037	Dar es Salaam	English; Swahili	Tanzanian shilling	29,058,000	5865 Kilimanjaro
Thailand	514,000	Bangkok	Thai	Baht	58,851,000	2595 Inthanon Mountain

Tables show a large amount of information in a small space. Unlike the information in other graphs, the information in tables does not all have to be the same kind. This table shows several kinds of information.

TABLE ATTACK!

Follow these steps to read a table.

1. Read the title. This table shows ____eight countries of the world____.
2. Read the words along the top and the left side of the table.

   a. What countries are shown in this table? __Brazil, Canada, Denmark,__

   __Egypt, Italy, New Zealand, Tanzania, Thailand__

   b. Name four pieces of information you can learn. Answers should include four of the following:

   area, capital, official language, unit of currency, population, or highest point.

3. Read the table.

   a. What is the largest country in area? ____Canada____

   b. What is the least populated country listed? ____New Zealand____

   c. What and where is the highest point listed? ____Mt. Logan, Canada____

4. Draw a conclusion.

   a. Which are the two largest countries in area? __Brazil__ __Canada__

   b. Which of those has the smaller population? ____Canada____

   c. Which has the greater population density? ____Brazil____

Comparing a Table and a Map

<table>
<tr><th colspan="5">Flights from Chicago</th></tr>
<tr><th>Departure
Time</th><th>Arrival
Time</th><th>Airline
Flight #</th><th colspan="2">Meal</th></tr>
<tr><td colspan="5">To Acapulco</td></tr>
<tr><td>8:55 AM</td><td>1:21PM</td><td>AA 169</td><td colspan="2">B</td></tr>
<tr><td>9:30 AM</td><td>3:15PM</td><td>MX 803</td><td colspan="2">LS</td></tr>
<tr><td colspan="5">To Bermuda</td></tr>
<tr><td>8:05 AM</td><td>3:40PM</td><td>DL 88</td><td colspan="2">BL</td></tr>
<tr><td colspan="5">To Calgary</td></tr>
<tr><td>10:00 AM</td><td>2:30PM</td><td>UA 933</td><td colspan="2">L</td></tr>
<tr><td>10:30 AM</td><td>3:00PM</td><td>AC 833</td><td colspan="2">L</td></tr>
<tr><td colspan="5">To Mexico City</td></tr>
<tr><td>1:50 AM</td><td>5:30AM</td><td>MX 181</td><td colspan="2">D</td></tr>
<tr><td>9:30 AM</td><td>1:10PM</td><td>MX 803</td><td colspan="2">L</td></tr>
<tr><td>3:45 PM</td><td>10:35PM</td><td>MX 815</td><td colspan="2">LS</td></tr>
<tr><td>9:50 PM</td><td>1:57AM</td><td>AA 57</td><td colspan="2">S</td></tr>
<tr><td colspan="5">To Milwaukee</td></tr>
<tr><td>7:00 AM</td><td>7:50AM</td><td>AA 1241</td><td colspan="2"></td></tr>
<tr><td>9:55 AM</td><td>10:31AM</td><td>UA 559</td><td colspan="2"></td></tr>
<tr><td>6:34 PM</td><td>7:16PM</td><td>AA 205</td><td colspan="2"></td></tr>
<tr><td colspan="5">To Montreal</td></tr>
<tr><td>7:10 AM</td><td>10:10AM</td><td>AA 696</td><td colspan="2">B</td></tr>
<tr><td>1:12 PM</td><td>4:12PM</td><td>AA 286</td><td colspan="2">S</td></tr>
<tr><td>5:40 PM</td><td>8:40PM</td><td>AA 410</td><td colspan="2">D</td></tr>
<tr><td>B - Breakfast
L - Lunch
S - Snack</td><td>D - Dinner
AA - American Airlines
AC - Air Canada</td><td colspan="3">DL - Delta Airlines
MX - Mexicana Airlines
UA - United Airlines</td></tr>
</table>

Time Zones in North America

1. Read the title.

   a. This table shows _____ flights from Chicago _____.

   b. The map shows _____ time zones in North America _____.

2. Read the words along the top and the left side of the table.

   a. The flights from Chicago are to _____ Acapulco, Bermuda, Calgary, Mexico City, Milwaukee, Montreal _____.

   b. What are two pieces of information you can learn about these flights? _____ Answers should include two of the following: departure time, arrival time, airline flight #, meal _____

3. Read the table key. What do the letters *AA* stand for? _____ American Airlines _____

   L? _____ lunch _____   *MX*? _____ Mexicana Airlines _____   *S*? _____ snack _____

4. Compare the table and the map.

   a. To which cities could you fly from Chicago without changing time zones? _____ Milwaukee, Acapulco, Mexico City _____

   b. How many time zones do you cross to fly from Chicago to Calgary? _1_

   c. If you left Chicago at 10:00 AM, what time would you arrive in Calgary? _____ 2:30 P.M. _____

   d. When you arrive in Calgary, what time is it in Chicago? _____ 3:30 P.M. _____

   e. How long was your trip? _____ 5½ hours _____

   f. How long is the trip from Chicago to Montreal? _____ 2 hours _____

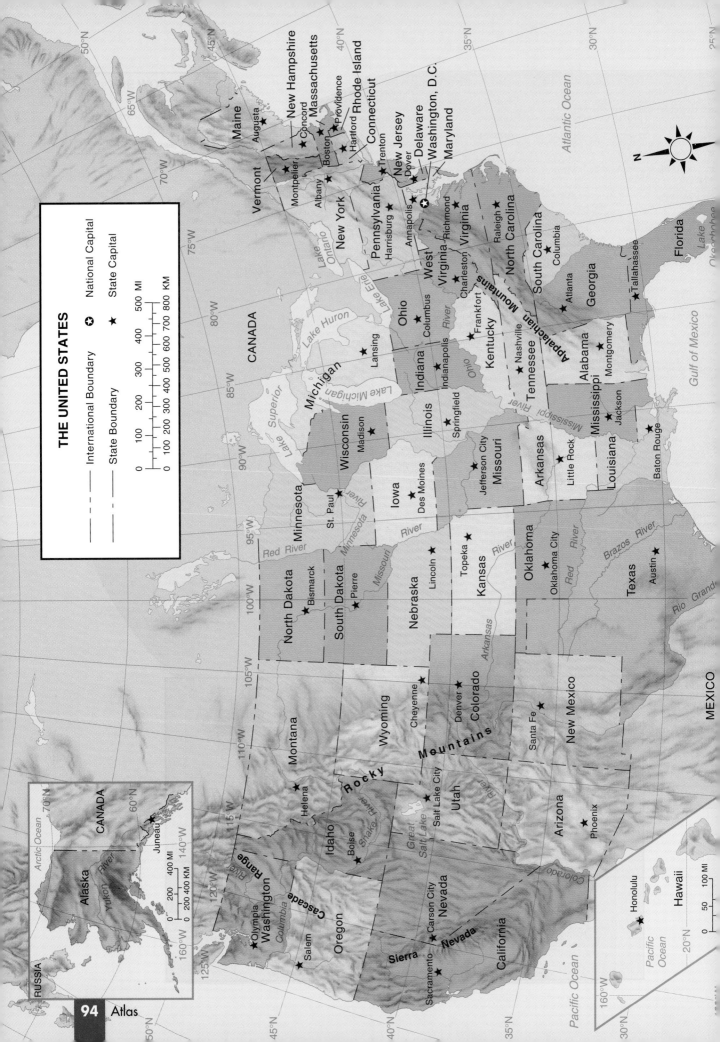

THE UNITED STATES

International Boundary
State Boundary

⊗ National Capital
★ State Capital

MI
0 100 200 300 400 500 MI
0 100 200 300 400 500 600 700 800 KM

Glossary

absolute location (p. 48)   the specific address or latitude and longitude coordinates of a place

Antarctic Circle (p. 50)   The parallel of latitude 66 ½° south of the Equator

Arctic Circle (p. 50)   the parallel of latitude 66 ½° north of the Equator

bar graph (p. 84)   a graph that uses thick bars of different lengths to compare numbers or amounts

cardinal directions (p. 14)   north, south, east, and west

cartographer (p. 78)   a mapmaker

charts (p. 21)   facts shown in columns and rows

circle graph (p. 86)   a graph that shows how something whole is divided into parts

climate (p. 50)   the average weather of a place over a long period of time

climate zone (p. 50)   an area with a generally similar climate

compass rose (p. 14)   a symbol that shows directions on a map

coordinates (p. 29)   the letter and number that identify a grid square; the latitude and longitude of a place

degrees (p. 42)   the units of latitude and longitude lines

desertification (p. 62)   the spread of desert conditions to neighboring areas

distortion (p. 78)   the changes in a sphere that are shown on a flat surface, such as a map

elevation (p. 37)   the height of land above the level of the sea

Equator (p. 8)   the imaginary line around the middle of Earth that divides Earth into the Northern and Southern Hemispheres

Frigid Zones (p. 50)   the high latitudes that are cold all year

geography (p. 4)   the study of Earth and the ways people use Earth

globe (p. 8)   a model of Earth shaped like a sphere or ball

grid (p. 29)   a pattern of lines that cross each other to form squares

hemisphere (p. 8)   half of a sphere; half of Earth; the four hemispheres are Eastern, Western, Northern, and Southern

high latitudes (p. 50)   the Frigid Zones north of the Arctic Circle and south of the Antarctic Circle that are cold all year

human/environment interaction (pp. 5, 62)   the ways that the environment affects people and people affect the environment

human features (p. 4)   features of a place or region made by people, such as population, jobs, language, customs, religion, and government

inset map (p. 23)   a small map within a larger map

interchange (p. 28)   a junction on a major highway with special connecting ramps to allow vehicles to change roads without interrupting the flow of traffic

intermediate directions (p. 14)   northeast, southeast, southwest, northwest

International Date Line (p. 71)   an imaginary line at about 180° longitude where the day changes

junction (p. 28)   a place where two highways cross or meet

kilometers (p. 22)   a unit of length used in measuring distance in the metric system

latitude (p. 42)   the distance north or south of the Equator measured in degrees

legend (p. 14)   a map key, or list of symbols on a map, and what they stand for

line graph (p. 88)   graph that shows how something changes over time

location (pp. 4, 48)   the absolute and relative position of people and places on Earth

longitude (p. 42)   the distance east or west of the Prime Meridian measured in degrees

low latitudes (p. 50) the tropics, or Torrid Zone, between the Tropic of Cancer and the Tropic of Capricorn that is warm all year

map index (p. 29) the alphabetical list of places on a map with their grid coordinates

map scale (p. 22) the guide that shows what distances on a map equal in the real world

Mercator projection (p. 79) a projection that shows the compass directions between places accurately. Distance and size are distorted, especially near poles.

meridians (p. 42) lines of longitude

middle latitudes (p. 50) the Temperate Zones between the high latitudes and low latitudes where weather changes from season to season

mileage markers (p. 28) small triangles and numbers on a map used to indicate distances along highways

miles (p. 22) a unit of length used in measuring distance

mouth (p. 36) the place where a river empties into a sea or ocean

movement (pp. 6, 20) how and why people, goods, information, and ideas move from place to place

North Pole (p. 8) the point farthest north on Earth

parallels (p. 42) lines of latitude

physical features (p. 4) natural features of a place or region, such as climate, landforms, soil, bodies of water, and plants and animals

place (pp. 4, 34) physical and human features of a location that make it different from other locations

polar projection (p. 79) a projection that is centered on one of the poles and shows the oceans and continents around the pole

population density (p. 57) the number of people living in a certain area

Prime Meridian (p. 42) the line of longitude from the North Pole to the South Pole and marked 0°

projection (p. 78) a way of showing Earth's curved surface on a flat map

reclaim (p. 63) to take back, such as land that has been flooded

regions (p. 7, 76) the basic unit of geography; areas that have one or more features in common

relative location (p. 48) describing a location by what it is near or what is around it

relief map (p. 36) a map that uses shading to show the elevation of land

Robinson projection (p. 79) the flat projection that most closely resembles a globe. It shows less distortion than other projections do.

source (p. 36) the place where a river begins

South Pole (p. 8) the point farthest south on Earth

standard time zones (p. 70) Earth is divided into 24 time zones. Each time zone has a clock time one hour earlier than the zone to its east.

Temperate Zones (p. 50) the middle latitudes where the weather changes from season to season

Torrid Zone (p. 50) the low latitudes, or tropics, that are warm all year round

tributaries (p. 36) rivers that flow into larger rivers

Tropic of Cancer (p. 50) the parallel of latitude $23\frac{1}{2}°$ north of the Equator

Tropic of Capricorn (p. 50) the parallel of latitude $23\frac{1}{2}°$ south of the Equator